More Than Liked

STAYING TRUE TO YOU IN A SOCIAL MEDIA-
OBSESSED GENERATION

Justin Burke

Author: Justin Burke
Title: More Than Liked / Justin Burke. —1st ed.
ISBN 978-0-692-08357-4

Contents

Your worth has nothing to do with your likes and follows. Whether you get zero likes or 10,000 likes, you're still the same amazing, uniquely gifted person who was created for something incredible.

Introduction

Wouldn't it be great to live above the drama and haters and never feel undervalued or overlooked? How about never worrying about how many likes you get on a pic or video compared to your friends? And wouldn't it be awesome to truly feel free to be yourself and enjoy having friends who like you for who you really are?

I wrote *More Than Liked: Staying True to You in a Social Media-Obsessed Generation* to tackle many of these tough issues we all face on a daily basis growing up in a social media-saturated generation. I've written the book as 30 daily readings, or short chapters, with a challenge and inspiration to focus on at the end of each. I hope you find the 30 daily readings enjoyable, easy to read, motivational, and encouraging, as well as super practical and helpful!

For those who might not know me, I'll quickly give you my story. I jumped on YouTube early (before it was YouTube as we know) when I was twelve, and I fell in love with creating content. That's also around the time I decided to start learning to sing and produce music, which led me to other platforms besides YouTube. To make a long story short, over time I've been blessed to build a social media community of over 1.5 million followers, and over 100 million views across my music and content, which has given me so many incredible experiences. If you've been a part of that, from the bottom of my heart, thank you!

During my journey, I have learned a lot. I've seen so much of the good that comes from social media, but I've also seen the bad. This new social media culture has incredible opportunities, but with those opportunities come dangerous traps we all need to avoid.

Over the years, I've received many messages dealing with the struggles our generation faces (myself included) and have responded to as many as I could. With so much social media content competing for our time and attention, I decided to put in print some things that have really helped me along my journey, in hopes they can encourage you on yours! All of us in our generation—no matter where we live—face similar challenges, so writing everything in one book seemed like a great idea to reach as many people as possible all at once.

I did my best to pack some powerful content for each day, so make sure you commit to doing the daily challenges at the end of each chapter! When you do them, you will feel the positive difference in your mindset and your day-to-day experience, because you'll be putting everything into actual practice in your life.

My goal for you is that by the end of the book, you will feel empowered, secure and confident in staying true to your best self and in who God created you to be...regardless of how many likes or dislikes, or followers or haters you have on social media. I also hope that genuine and lasting happiness will increase in your heart to the point where it spills out to those around you, both online and offline. And as you read each chapter and daily challenge, I hope you will be encouraged and inspired to live your life with purpose and passion, and be a blessing to others along the way, knowing your uniqueness is making a difference.

Together we can turn the tide and use social media for

good in our relationships and influence, and be the positive change our world needs!

Will you join me? Let's do this!

All the best :),

Justin

CHAPTER 1

Live Your Unique Journey

God has a unique plan for our lives, and we need to be faithful to that unique plan.

Have you ever felt like you get distracted following other people's journeys and neglect your own? With millions of people to watch and so many social media platforms to view, it's literally overwhelming! Even though it is super fun to check out and enjoy other people's talents and creativity, and even get inspired by them, it's all too easy to get lost in other people's lives and follow them only to compare yourself to their perceived successes.

You may or may not have felt this way, but for me personally, it's been a journey for me to get to a place where I don't get sucked into looking at others (especially on social media) and what they are doing in relation to me. This leads to thinking things like, "Why am I not ahead in my career like they are?" "Why don't I look like him?" "Why can't I have that house, that car, that relationship, etc.?" "Why don't I have it all figured out?!" I bet you can relate at one time or another.

What I came to realize is that I have no reason to spend my valuable time and energy obsessing over what other people are doing! It makes no sense. I believe that God has a unique plan for your life and my life, and we need to be faithful to that unique plan. That is the best place to be! (Like Abe Lincoln encouraged his colleague, *God's way is fail-proof*.) You are the only one that can do what God has specifically created you to do!

Everything happens for a reason. Not trying to be cliché, but it's the absolute truth. Trust me when I say, there is no need to try and rush God's plan. *You are not in a race with anyone except yourself.* The only person you should compare yourself to is who you were yesterday, no one else. It is your own race you are running, with a pace that is fit for your unique purpose and plan. And the way to win the race is to be faithful to your unique, God-given journey, building other people up along the way in theirs. That is where real happiness and fulfillment are found.

Now don't get me wrong, anyone that knows me personally knows I'm all about getting things done and actively pursuing my dreams—putting in work and making it happen (ask my roommates...they know how I can burn the midnight oil)! But, sometimes I can get so obsessed with desiring the end goal (or wishing to be like someone else I see who has what I think I want) that the whole idea becomes overwhelming, and *I lose the motivation to even start.* Ever felt that way?

A Chinese proverb says, *The longest journey starts with a single step.* When you're ready to start pursuing your dreams, you have to stop spending time looking at others, and just start moving forward step by step. It's your life, it's your unique journey, and you are right where you are supposed to be at this moment! Because the truth is, it doesn't matter where you are right now, *what matters is where you decide to go from here.* The key is to *just get started.*

Whatever it is you want to do, whether in school, athletics, relationships, work, building a business, cultivating a community on social media, or anything that involves effort—learn to love the process, because achieving the outcome will require lots of patience. You might as well enjoy the ride!

Let me be real with you, when I first began creating my own music back in my early teens, as far as what most of the world would say... I failed—badly! (Of course my mom always thought I was great, ha!) But as with most things in life, we will rarely (if ever) be great on our first try. In fact, a lot of my friends made fun of me for trying to sing and create music, and even though that was really disappointing to me, *I didn't let it stop me from learning.* I turned their disbelief into a motivator for me to continue learning! I would spend hours training my voice, hours writing songs, hours learning to produce and edit films, and hours promoting my music.

Over the years, I have had to push through so many failed ideas and numerous rejections. Keep in mind that you might too...but actually be glad for the failures, because that is how you learn and grow. Did you know that Michael Jordan didn't make his high school varsity basketball team one year while his classmate took the spot, and Walt Disney was actually fired at a newspaper for not having very good ideas? Crazy!! These guys are admired all over the world for the very things they "failed" in at first!

As I faced my failures, the positive changes didn't happen overnight. I remember my first live performance years ago, it was in front of all my friends. I was literally shaking before going up; I almost felt like my throat closed up. (If you can't tell yet, I was super nervous!) And to make things worse, I totally cracked on the high note of the song. It seems hilarious now looking back, but I was so embarrassed at the time. I wanted to quit and never embarrass myself like that again. But I forced myself to keep at it, and after several times, I felt so much more comfortable—which freed me up to sing my best and actually enjoy it too.

Honestly, every notable achievement I have experienced and have watched others attain have come with periods of struggle, which actually have given opportunity for refinement and growth. With the music, it took hours of work each day, over multiple years, before I got any kind of traction (and I had to continue working, even when no one was paying me much attention). That sounds like a lot of time, but it goes by so fast when you stop comparing yourself to others, and focus on improving day by day, moving forward, step by step. To be real, looking back, it was actually a ton of fun even the struggles—when I finally stopped *comparing* and fell in love with the process of *growing*.

Taking on a big goal takes persistence and lots of time and patience, so if you can learn to love doing the little things that grow you as a person day by day, it will produce big results over time! I've become so much happier and confident in who I am when I finally decided to put the blinders on and not compare so much to what others are doing, but fall in love with *my own journey*... fall in love with pursuing the path that I believe God has for *me*. I encourage you to do the same for you, since life becomes so much more exciting and fun. Above all, remember, run your own race!

DAILY CHALLENGE:

Get those blinders on (stop comparing your path to others)! Take time today to plan out your ideal vision for yourself and your unique journey, and proactively take steps each day to achieve your goals, whatever they might be. Start by writing down three things you could do each day to move you closer to where you want to be. It won't happen overnight, or maybe not even this year, but if you stay faithful to the passion God has put inside you, it will happen when the time is right. And when the timing is right for you to break out, you will be ready, because you've put the work in, and you'll have grown in the process.

DAILY INSPIRATION:

Let us strip off every weight that slows us down...and let us run with endurance the race God has set before us. (Hebrews 12:1 NLT)

CHAPTER 2

What To Do If You're Getting Hate

Don't ever let haters destroy the God-given passion within you!

E veryone has an opinion. Haters are always going to hate. It's inevitable! And since social media is opened up to the entire globe, there are millions of haters out there spewing hate out! So don't feel badly for getting some of it.

To this day, for every ten comments, I'll get at least one to two negative ones (especially if the video goes viral). When you put yourself out there, you're going to get some negative opinions. Unfortunately, it's just the world we live in. Like Aristotle said thousands of years ago, the only way to avoid criticism is to be nothing, do nothing, or say nothing! And obviously no one can live that way, nor would anyone want to.

I remember when I first opened up a YouTube account

when I was almost twelve. I started to put up fun content, grew pretty fast, and then after a few months, people began to make accounts with names like "JustinBurkeSucks," and much more explicit names, ha! Can you believe that? It's crazy how some people go through all the trouble just to dislike videos and leave ridiculously mean comments. Looking back, it's pretty funny, but my twelve-year-old self didn't think so. Even though I was having fun being creative, and I got positive feedback from some really nice viewers, the hate that I was getting honestly felt devastating at the time.

Trust me, if you feel like you are getting a lot of hate or negativity aimed towards you right now, you are not alone. And I'll be real, it hurts. Hateful comments have really hurt me in the past, and even though it's gotten easier, I know there will be times I will still be hurt by them.

Just remember: *Hate may hurt you, but it can't stop you*! You can't let hate stop you from pursuing your dreams. If you quit because of other people's hateful opinions, you let hate win! God put you in this world for a purpose, and God has put a passion inside of you. Don't ever let hate or negativity destroy, block, or crush that passion!

When I was younger, I let hate get the best of me. After about a year of creating music on YouTube, I was gaining serious traction and opportunities were opening up, which were really awesome. Everything I had been working so hard for was finally coming into place. But I was getting tons of hate at the same time, like I mentioned earlier. And sadly, I let the haters win. I quit releasing music. I quit making videos. The hate got to me. I came back after a few years, but it was too late for some of the opportunities. The opportunities had come and gone.

Quitting during that time was one of the biggest mistakes

I have ever made. I literally vowed to myself to never give up on my dreams again due to negative people or haters. I've stuck to it ever since, and thankfully, God has given me new opportunities that have replaced those I lost. And He will do that for you, too, as you focus on your plan and not the haters' plan for your life!

Here's what I've come to realize: If someone is hating on you, it has nothing to do with you at all—*it's about them*! Ah, I wish I knew this when I was younger. Truthfully, haters feel jealous or inferior to you in some way, and the only way they can cope with this feeling is to try to bring you down to their level. Haters gave up on their dreams, and watching you actively pursue yours triggers them.

On the other hand, another reason for the hate might be because the person is really struggling, and they are just taking their anger out on you. As I've grown up, my parents always taught me that hurt people *hurt people*. Get it? People that have been hurt without healing from it often turn around and hurt others to hide from their pain. Nevertheless, *it has nothing to do with you*. As crazy as it sounds, *pray* for your haters! That's what I do now. And believe it or not, this actually changes my perspective from being *hurt* to being *hopeful* that my prayers will make a difference in their lives for the better.

Another important point I want to touch on is this: Stop worrying about what others may think when they see hate on your posted content. When I get hate on my content, or see it on anyone else's, I feel sad for the haters, never for the creators. I feel embarrassed for the haters, never for the person sharing content that has a rude comment on their page. I translate a negative comment to, "I am hurting so badly emotionally that I can't bear to see others having fun and sharing creativity." That's literally what I read in my mind when I see any form of negativity toward another person. That doesn't mean that the hate won't hurt, but it does help put things into perspective.

That being said, you should still get the nasty and negative stuff off of your social media page as soon as you are aware it is there. You owe these people nothing, and have absolutely no obligation to leave their comments up. Block them to prevent more negativity, and remove the comments. Do it in a classy way (by this I mean don't be hateful back or respond in anger, since that is stooping to their level). Just know that hateful or inappropriate comments have no place polluting your social media page, or anyone's for that matter, so remove them.

Haters are in desperate need of help to grow as people and reach their full potential, and praying for them reminds me of that. Plus, they need God's love to overcome that hurt and hate. Keep in mind, you can increase the love represented on social media by posting kind and encouraging words on other people's posts, drowning out hateful comments

Focus on the best, not the worst. Focus on what you can praise, not curse. Let's put our energy toward being the positive change we want to see in this world! You'll be amazed how even the smallest act of kindness can make the biggest difference in someone's life.

DAILY CHALLENGE:

Today, promise yourself to never let negativity lead you to give up on your dreams. If you get hate or negative comments, tell yourself "this is about them, not about me," and wish them the best as you delete their comment. Go through your posts and delete hateful comments people have made (as well as delete any negative comments you may have carelessly posted on others' content). Of course, hate will always hurt a little, but let it go immediately, and definitely don't let it stop you! When you have haters, use it as an opportunity to love your enemies, and watch how it grows you in the process.

DAILY INSPIRATION:

But I say, love your enemies! Pray for those who persecute you! In that way, you will be acting as true children of your Father in heaven. ~Jesus (Matthew 5:44-45 NLT)

CHAPTER 3

You are More Than Liked

Whether you get zero likes or 10,000 likes, you're still the same amazing, uniquely gifted person who was created for something incredible.

"*How many likes did my post get today? Only three?! Okay something must be wrong. Did I not sing well? Do I not look good? Does anyone actually care? Ah, I lost ten followers. Okay, I definitely need to delete this post. This is embarrassing. I guess no one actually cares.*" And the day is ruined...

That scenario might be a little extreme to make a point, but I believe we can all relate to it to a certain degree. Basically, it's easy to get your worth as a person tied up with your popularity on social media. I know I can relate to that.

I'll be honest, in the past, my notifications on social media have really toyed with my mood. People that unfollowed me have really messed with me. Because it takes serious effort to put out content, I really want people to like what I post. But in the past, I've felt like a part of my worth as a person somehow got tangled up in social media numbers along the way, and that was an endless cycle of frustration with so many people to please.

Sounds silly writing it out, but it's true. And I believe this is so important to discuss in this book, because I have received so many messages from others dealing with the same thing. We are not alone in feeling this way.

And I'll also add that all the top "social media stars" deal with this too. We are all the same. In fact, it's almost as if the more attention you get, the more insecure you become about it. The feeling doesn't go away with increased popularity. Once you get 10,000, you want 50,000. Once you get 50,000 you want 500,000, and so on. Trust me, the insecurity isn't solved by more popularity or fame.

Here's the thing—it is totally normal to want people to like what we do, and that is natural and not a problem by itself. But having our *worth as a person* get caught up in our "likes" is definitely a problem. Having our self-worth tied to other people's opinions never ends well. With social media this really becomes magnified, and even more dangerous to our well-being, if we are unaware of how to temper it.

Here's the crazy truth I've come to realize: No one is thinking long and hard about you or how you look. Not that people don't care about you as a person, but honestly, they are really mainly thinking about themselves! They are thinking about all the same insecure thoughts you're thinking about. They're not thinking about what you are worried they're thinking. Why? Because they are thinking more about how they are coming across to *you.* They have their own insecurities they are worried about, they don't have time to notice yours. Just like you don't have time to notice everything about them.

The more experience I get, the more irony I find in one of our most difficult insecurities to conquer—the fear of what others think. I've come to this conclusion: *Everyone is spending time worrying about what everyone else thinks of them when they actually aren't thinking about anyone else but themselves!* Yet, we so often view ourselves the way we *think* others are viewing us, but we have no idea what is actually going on in their heads. (I would bet it has nothing to do with us.) Are you following me? It's just a recipe for disaster. Once you fully understand this truth, it becomes irrational to base your self-worth on perceived outside opinions.

I'll be real with you, when I was younger, what you thought of me was one of my biggest insecurities. In high school, I felt like I struggled with it more than anyone. I spent hours contemplating whether people would like a song I wrote, video I filmed, vlog I posted, photo I took...the list goes on. But if I judge my value based on counting the number of my "likes," it is harmful to me.

The honest truth is, the only "like" that matters is God's, and He *loves* you, so that tops them all. When we find our worth solely in the fact that we were created by God for a wonderful purpose, it really makes no difference how many likes or followers we have on our posts, does it?

Easy to say, I know, and I wish I could say I am totally free from it now. I'm not. But I'm getting there, and I can honestly say I spend way less time worrying about likes than I did, which has definitely freed me up to be more content, confident and happy online and offline.

Because in truth, when it comes down to it, there is really nothing to worry about! No one actually cares about our insecurities like we do. We need to give ourselves a break from the pressure we put on ourselves. Again, I'm not saying that people don't care about us, but they don't care about our insecurities like we think. How freeing is that?

Let me end with one more important point. Your image or popularity online or offline does not define who you are. Your worth has nothing to do with your likes and follows. Whether you get zero likes or 10,000 likes, you're still the same amazing, uniquely gifted person who was created for something incredible. Remember, social media apps are basically just games on your phone that could be gone tomorrow—they do *not* define you! You are *so much more than liked*, never forget that!

DAILY CHALLENGE:

Understand that *your image or popularity online or offline does not define who you are.* If you are starting to find yourself constantly checking your likes and follows, or feeling inadequate as a person if you aren't getting the amount of activity on social media you want, I recommend taking a break from checking your notifications. You'll find that after a few days of not checking notifications, your activity on social media won't affect you nearly as much. At the end of the day, social media apps have nothing to do with your worth as a person. You are *so much more than liked!*

DAILY INSPIRATION:

God never overlooks a single one. And he pays even greater attention to you, down to the last detail—even numbering the hairs on your head! So don't be intimidated...You're worth more than a million... ~Jesus (Luke 12:6-7 MSG)

CHAPTER 4

Build Friends Not Followers

It's important to remind ourselves that social media was created for community — to bring us closer, not farther apart.

You realize how lucky we all are? We are all living in a time like no other. We have access to a global community directly from our phone. It's unreal if you really stop and think about it!

Ten years ago, it wasn't possible to share a group chat with friends from different countries and cultures at the same time. So many opportunities have opened up through social media that were never available to other generations. Opportunities to pursue new dreams and the ability to live and communicate with friends globally are accessible to practically anyone with a cell phone.

Social media is an amazing tool, yet sadly sometimes we don't use it correctly. Although it was created to bring us all together, sometimes it feels like it pushes us further apart. To be real, at times my time spent on social media has caused me loneliness and isolation. At the end of the day, it's important to remind ourselves that social media was created for community. It was created to bring us closer, not farther apart.

No doubt, living in community is vital to our happiness. Let's be real, life can be extremely tough, and we need each other's support to get through it. Social media can seriously help with this, if approached in a way that encourages positivity and community.

Sometimes, the people in your geographic location might not be the best of friends. They might not provide the support you need, or in some cases, people that live near you may be the cause of a lot of pain. Here's the good news. With social media, you can find (or create) that supportive community you might not have locally, and you can enjoy community this way while continuing to look for others in your area whom you can trust.

I've spent a lot of time cultivating supportive relationships with others on social media. It's been life-changing for me. Over time, I've built a community based around encouragement. Now, when I'm feeling stressed, if I don't have family and friends nearby, I know I can also reach out to my friends online. I can get support when I'm discouraged, and give support to others too. It's allowed me to build deep friendships from all around the world. This is social media at its best!

On the flip side, social media is a waste of time if it's just used for showing off, judging others, or spending hours per day wasting time browsing random people's feeds we will never actually engage with. I've definitely fallen into that trap. If the goal of using social media is not relationships, but just to feel "cool" and "popular," trust me, that is a really lonely journey—and I've been there too.

At the end of the day, never lose sight of the fact that time spent on social media should be used to enhance your feeling of community with others, not enhance isolation! The time spent on social media (away from our friends offline) should be used to build supportive relationships and cultivate a community of like-minded friends.

Having people I can go to, either online or offline, that can celebrate with me in the awesome times, or give emotional support when times are tough, has been incredible to cultivate and totally worth the investment. Life isn't meant to be experienced alone, the good or the bad! And you don't have to either. We are in this together.

I'll always remember how touched I was to receive a package in the mail my freshman year of college. Two of my online friends who have supported me from the early days (when I first began broadcasting and sharing my music on social media) coordinated an effort to gather letters from over a hundred of my other social media friends and supporters from all over the world.

These incredible people sent in letters to my two friends, telling me how much I had helped them or encouraged them or walked with them through a dark time. Then my friends packaged all the letters, tied each with a blue ribbon (knowing blue is my favorite color), put them in a big glass jar and mailed it to me. They did all this so I would know that I had made a difference in all these people's lives, no matter what happens in the future with my career. I tear up thinking about it. That goes down as one of the most meaningful things anyone has ever done for me.

You see, although all these friends didn't know, I was going through a really tough time at that point, and the letters were such a gift to me. Through their kindness, God reminded me that I was still making a difference. I have those letters in a special place, and I still read them, and my heart is encouraged every time. Those letters are a constant reminder to stay focused on the passion God has put inside me, and to value and lift people up along the way.

The cool thing is that many of the people that sent in letters from all over the world had met and become great friends through my online community. The two that pulled off the awesome surprise for me even met each other that way, living in two different countries, but still becoming super close friends.

There are people out there who get you, and who will appreciate you for the amazing person you are. They would love to support you! Don't worry about those that don't, because there are even more who do, and God will lead you to like-minded friends who will value you like He does. Don't give the others any more of your time!

So, if you are feeling alone, and you can't seem to find supportive friendship in your local area, I encourage you to join a caring online community. Use social media to find that community or even create it yourself! Some easy ways to do this include setting up a group chat or Skype, Facebook group, or using a group app. Use social media for what it is meant for—building genuine community and friendships. Accept nothing less. :)

DAILY CHALLENGE:

Today, find at least three people to proactively encourage. Let this act as a seed planted to grow your community of friends. If you feel like no one gets you in your local area, find a positive, supportive community online you can jump into (while continuing to search out and build meaningful friendships locally). Instead of surfing the Explore page on social media for hours, use that time to begin building your own community group.

DAILY INSPIRATION:

So encourage each other and build each other up, just as you are already doing. (1 Thessalonians 5:11 NLT)

CHAPTER 5

Forgive and Let Go

Forgiveness will set you free.

You might be surprised at one of the most asked questions I get, and it has nothing to do with singing or songwriting. It's actually a part of the reason why I wrote this book. It's about needing advice on how to deal with hurt and pain from comments made on social media or from friends in person that have been hurtful.

I get so many messages from people telling me that they've been hurt by someone else (on social media or in person), or that they wished they wouldn't have posted, messaged or said what they did, and it is really affecting them mentally. If that's you, you are not alone; I've definitely been there too. It's safe to say we have all been there. The first step to feeling better is forgiveness. *Forgiveness will set you free.*

Here's the thing: We have a finite amount of willpower and limited mental energy to use throughout the day. It makes no sense to let negative people or past mistakes rob you of your precious energy. If you get a hateful comment, forgive whoever commented. This doesn't mean you have to be their friend, but don't let them take up any more of your mental energy. Don't give them that power. When people hate on others, whether online or offline, they just want to get a response or reaction. Don't give that to them!

This relates directly to social media, but forgiveness should be a part of every area of your life. It's a way of life. Several years ago, I had one of my close friends completely turn his back on me out of nowhere. He said some really negative and hurtful stuff about me, to others I knew, to his parents, even to my parents, then finally to my face. Sad part is, the worst of it wasn't true. To be honest with you, it felt like I was betrayed by someone I cared so deeply about. It definitely hurt to the core when this happened.

For months, the situation controlled my mind. Ever felt that way? My mind would spin around wondering, "Why?", "How?" And the things I should have said, things I should have done, spun in my thoughts. I was letting negativity win; my energy was being drained. I had to learn to forgive even when it felt like every part of me told me not to. I had to realize that it did me absolutely no good thinking about what happened, why it happened, or fantasizing ways to get revenge. That just poisoned my spirit.

I learned a lot from the situation, and it taught me how to forgive when I didn't necessarily want to. It doesn't mean we're great friends again or that we hang out, but I am free from the hurt and feeling happy again, and hopefully they can say the same thing. Forgiveness is freeing!

Forgiveness transcends beyond just forgiving our haters— forgiving ourselves is just as important. We all make mistakes. We have to admit them, and grow from them. As my dad likes to say, "No perfect people allowed." If we pretend to be perfect, we will never grow. What matters is our attitude moving forward. If you feel like you made a mistake... like let's just say you messaged or DM'd something you wish you hadn't. Do the right thing and apologize first, make it right as far as it depends on you, then forgive yourself. It's okay. Take action to improve for next time and ask for forgiveness where needed, but beyond that, let it go.

I don't know what your personal beliefs are, but I respect them, and I'm going to share mine. What helps me forgive is realizing how much I've been forgiven by God—past, present, and future. I've done, said, or thought plenty of wrong things that I knew were not God's will. Yet God forgives me and doesn't condemn, so I should also forgive myself. I believe Jesus came and died and rose again to pay for all humanity's wrongs, so we can know God forgives. That way, we can forgive others and ourselves, because God forgives and will help us do the same for others.

You can't write a new beginning, but you can write a new ending. The past is the past, you can't change it. But you can keep your focus on the future, for that's the only path forward. Cultivating forgiveness is essential if you want to stay true to your best self on social media, but it's also necessary for living your best life in general.

Let's be real, we all let each other down. I understand it's difficult at times, but if we could all just learn to forgive others and ourselves, the world would be a much better place. Let's be the generation that makes a positive difference in the world by making forgiveness and love a priority!

DAILY CHALLENGE:

Write down at least three things that have been weighing you down mentally. This could be situations, people, yourself, whatever. Write down at least one thing you can learn from that negative situation, then forgive whomever or whatever you need to...including yourself. Let it go. Don't let the situation weigh you down any longer. Feel how incredibly freeing it is to *forgive.*

DAILY INSPIRATION:

Lord, you are so good, so ready to forgive, so full of unfailing love for all who ask for your help. (Psalm 86:5)

CHAPTER 6

Create What You Love

Create content that brings you joy—you are created to be creative!

Creating content on social media that brings you joy and makes you happy is the best feeling. I'm talking about the kind of content where the viewers really get to know the real you. There is such a freedom that comes from being real. No doubt, I'd take *real* over *cool* any day! Knowing deep down that people like you for you, and all that comes with that, feels *really* good.

Like most of us, I remember days when I would try to be "cool," whatever that means. I would act certain ways around certain people so that I could get their approval, or for them to like me. Can you relate? I think people of all ages deal with this in one way or another. From my experience, I found that even if I got people's approval, at the end of the day, I just felt even more lonely. I felt like no one really knew me. So I finally decided to give up "coolness" and "popularity" and just be me! I discovered I would rather have a few people really love me for me, with all my imperfections, than put on a mask to win everyone's approval. And I have to say it was the best feeling being myself and finding friends that I liked to be around, and who genuinely liked me too! How freeing that was!

Social media can feel like a popularity contest at times, including posting what we think our friends would like to see more, or trying to portray an image that we think will get more people to follow (even if it is inauthentic). *Warning!!* This is a path toward un-fulfillment, and it will likely head straight to frustration and burnout.

And let's be honest, we can all tell what is created just to get more eyeballs, and what is created out of an authentic love for the creation. Inauthenticity is obvious. We know what looks contrived, and can spot "clickbait" for views in a heartbeat.

Let me take you a few years back... When I was first starting out, as most first-time YouTubers do, I was obsessed with getting more views, more subscribers, more you-name-it! I would watch what other popular creators were doing, and I would try to copy that to get similar views.

Now this isn't necessarily a bad thing; it is actually a good way to see what content people like to watch as well as get ideas from people that like to create similar stuff as you. But taken to extreme measures, it can be over-the-top and actually not be content you enjoy creating at all!

I'll never forget the days as a thirteen-year-old creator. I'd be looking at leaked song sites or breaking news sites to be the first to post with the keywords in my title to get the most views. Totally ridiculous! I was clickbait king back in the day—before clickbait was a thing! Sure, some of the posts got millions of plays, but I wasn't proud of the content—so, what's the point if tons of people see it?

Okay, I'll share something really embarrassing with you, so don't tell anyone... I clearly remember creating one video in particular. It was a parody of a song that just leaked and hadn't been released. Wanting to capitalize on the views, I totally rushed the video. It involved off-tempo lip-syncing with a pink wig in a hot tub. (Are you cringing yet?) That's just a bad combination! This was three months ago... *kidding!* Even though it was six or seven years ago, I remember it so clearly. I posted the video up on YouTube with a thumbnail of the artist—*total clickbait.*

The video ended up getting over a million views, but the content wasn't great, I didn't enjoy creating it, and I wasn't proud of it (and the comment section definitely agreed with me, ha!). I shouldn't have worried about views, and instead created a video I enjoyed, one that I would have *wanted* a million people to see! Now, don't get me wrong, even though I share that with you as something not to do, I have to say I had fun back in the day as I explored my creative boundaries. And you can too! But if your thing is building an audience, just make sure you are *proud of what you create!*

The point is, the goal should never be views and likes. Everything I've ever put out to the world with the intention of "looking really cool" or "getting tons of views" never turns out as well as the ones I genuinely work hard on and am proud of creating. People see through it anyway, but most importantly, it doesn't make you feel good if it doesn't reflect the real you.

You are uniquely creative, let that creativity shine! You and I are created to be creative! We can create cool stuff simply from our imaginations. When you create from deep in your heart, in a way that is unique and authentic to you, regardless of what others are doing, that's what everyone wants to see. When you're thinking about what kind of content you want to put out to the world, just focus on what inspires you the most, and what can serve the most people, and the right audience will come.

Now just to be clear—this does *not* mean to be a perfectionist about what you put up. Embrace the imperfections! God created you with such a wonderful uniqueness—no one else can compare. Your "imperfections" are what make you! Don't worry about what other people are going to think of what you're creating. If it reflects the passion inside you, go for it! Here's the summation, *as long as you enjoy creating it, you're proud of the creation, and you believe it could benefit others, post it up!*

DAILY CHALLENGE:

Today, or the next time you post on social media, whether a photo, a video, a vlog, or whatever it may be, choose something that reflects the true you and the creativity God has put inside you. Steer away from creating a copy of others' posts, or what you think people want to see. Create something that is true to you.

DAILY INSPIRATION:

God has given each of you a gift from his great variety of spiritual gifts. Use them well to serve one another. (1 Peter 4:10 NLT)

CHAPTER 7

Give What You Wish to Receive

There is an immense amount of happiness and joy found in giving value to another person without expecting anything in return.

I think it is safe to say that every human being desires to be known, loved, and enjoyed by true friends. It doesn't matter if you are an introvert or an extrovert, shy or out-going—friends are important!

In high school, there were times when I didn't feel close to anyone at all. I felt it was difficult for me to build close re-lationships with friends my age. At times, I just felt so lonely. All I could think about is why others weren't relating to me the way I wished they would. I wanted close friends so bad-ly—I didn't understand why I felt so distant and lonely from everyone.

Have you caught my problem yet? It took me awhile, but I finally caught it too. The reason I couldn't find close friends was because I was focused only on *finding* them. Kind of confusing, right? Basically, my attention was on *receiving* friendship rather than *giving* it.

I wasn't focused on being the kind of friend I wanted in my life. As soon as I began to focus on how I could *be* a good friend, by taking interest in others and serving those around me, the friends I had tried to find started to come into my life. No joke—it's crazy how that works! Give what you wish to receive. By becoming the friend I wished I had to other people, I attracted those same kinds of friends into my life. Who would have thought!?

I'll give another example that relates to social media. When I first started posting on social media, my original goal was to push my music out into the world. But of course, at first, no one seemed to care or pay much attention to what I was doing. I was putting in so much effort, but I wasn't making progress. Then I started thinking, "I'll bet others are feeling the same way I am, so I'm going to go do for others what I wish people were doing for me." I started visiting other people's channels, seeing the awesome content that some were posting, and leaving encouraging comments on their feed when I really enjoyed what they posted. Basically, I gave to others what I wished I had. And over time, people started returning the support. Again, give what you wish to receive.

Deep down, we all just want to know that people care. Likewise, we can pick up quickly on the vibes when we feel people are "using" us. On social media, I support the people whom I feel truly care about their followers and know that their followers are real people (and not just numbers to boost their "likes" and "follows"). Same story with my personal relationships. I want to be friends with people that genuinely care about me, but also who value others and find ways to be a blessing. Don't you feel the same?

Our relationships won't last if we are only trying to take support without ever giving it. If I need to ask a favor from my friends, I always ask myself, "Have I given value or worth to this person in the form of my time, energy, encouragement, loyalty, etc.?" I try to make sure I am treating others the way I wish to be treated as best I can. I'm not perfect with this, but it's always something I strive for. I definitely encourage you to do the same. It is such a great feeling to know you are building someone up and helping them feel good about themselves!

So, if you want to create stronger personal relationships, the secret is *giving first*—words of encouragement, acts of service, prayer support, your time, a listening ear. It's not difficult at all. Not only is giving important for your emotional well-being, but it's the secret to facilitating positive relationships with the people around you.

Here's what else I've discovered: There is an immense amount of happiness and joy found in giving value to another person *without expecting anything in return*. Who would have thought? Not only will it make you feel incredible, but you just become magnetic. People want to be around you!

I'll be real though, this can be tough to do sometimes. Definitely easier for me to write about than to actually put into practice. When you shift to a mindset of giving first, keep yourself in check to make sure you are not giving only to get something in return. Giving with an agenda of getting something in return kills the joy you can be receiving from choosing unconditional kindness.

In a weird way of looking at it, the most selfish thing we can do for ourselves is live with unconditional kindness and love! It takes the focus off of our own problems, and fills our spirit with the joy that comes from helping others. Plus, we never know when someone is emotionally lost at sea, struggling to survive, and reaching out a hand to help could be life-saving for them.

This mindset can also make a positive difference in other important areas in our lives. For instance, most of the times I have felt anxious or really down on myself, I can trace back to when I was over-thinking about my inadequacies. Personally, I'm always the happiest when I take the focus off of myself and my personal problems (I've got a lot, trust me), and put my focus on others and how I can better serve and help them with theirs.

Let's relate this back to social media now. Giving value on social media can come in all different forms. A few examples might be: sharing our passions in a way that inspires others, offering encouraging ideas, frequently checking in on friends and genuinely caring about how they are doing, and supporting others who are doing good for our global community.

Sometimes, people won't give back to us in the same way, but that's all good. Don't worry about it, keep giving! What I've come to realize is this: *It's not about getting anything in return, it's all about the freedom and joy you receive from loving others unconditionally.*

DAILY CHALLENGE:

Today, post at least five encouraging comments on your friends' social media pages. Think of something really meaningful to them that will brighten up their day (other than just "great pic," "niceeee," etc.). If you want to take it a step further, text a few of your closest friends and tell them how much they mean to you. Start building the habit of giving first, with unconditional kindness, not expecting anything in return, and watch your friendships grow.

DAILY INSPIRATION:

Do to others whatever you would like them to do to you. ~Jesus (Matthew 7:12 NLT)

CHAPTER 8

What Would Love Do?

Just because we are online doesn't mean we have an excuse to be rude or hurtful; we are still responsible to treat others with the same respect and kindness all human beings deserve.

As amazing as social media is, it can be a dangerous place for some people. Because it brings a real feeling of anonymity, some feel they can get away with anything. Like I mentioned, people tend to say and do things online that they would never do in person. Because of the so-called "protection" behind the keyboard, some people tend to feel they can cross ethical boundaries that truly should not be crossed. This is so important in our social media generation. We all need to be reminded that everyone has feelings online, just as they do offline in person.

I am so grateful for all the encouragement I get in my comment streams. I have the most loyal and encouraging online friends! I want you all to know how much I appreciate every kind and affirming comment you write. However, sometimes I'll get the most ridiculously hateful comments from the most random people. Yet, to this date, I've never had a random person walk up to me and tell me to "**** myself" like I get online. Hopefully it stays that way!

But thinking about it this way is a good motivator to keep a check on our own texts and comments, and make sure we don't speak any differently on social media than we would to the person directly. Just because we are online doesn't mean we have an excuse to be rude or hurtful. We are still responsible to treat others with the same respect and kindness all human beings deserve.

It is crucial to be careful of your actions toward others online. Not only for your emotional well-being and theirs, but also because of the real world consequences. The protection you might feel behind the keyboard isn't actually protection at all. What you do online has a real effect on real people, with real consequences. And I don't just mean between you and another person. Given the infraction, it can really get you in a big mess. Keep in mind that messages and content are being saved and can be recovered, even if you deleted them on your end.

Let me give a personal example of how Internet privacy is an illusion. I remember several years ago one of my family members got hacked on Facebook, and the hacker was messaging really inconsiderate things from my family member's account posing as my family member, and we could see in the message stream that the hacker was trying to lure private information out of the person. Fortunately, a friend, who was visiting at the time, happened to be a really smart tech guy, and intervened to help.

After a few hours, we were able to get the account back,

and communicated to the person who was being tricked that a hacker had been messaging him, and not my family member. But the craziest thing was that our savvy tech friend was able to find everything out about who the hacker was, even down to their exact house about fifteen miles away. Sounds impossible? Nope, it was actually pretty easy for our friend to find. We peacefully worked the situation out, but our hacker could have been in deep trouble with the law had we pushed it forward.

The consequences on social media are real. I'm not at all trying to scare you about it, but I want to raise your awareness to it. It's obvious that many people still post and message carelessly. So, if you are not being careful enough, please start now! I'd hate to see a careless post close opportunities for you down the road. (I'll talk about this in more detail in a future chapter.)

Luckily, it's an easy fix to keep from getting caught up in a mess. Just do your best to love others in all that you do, online and offline. Be respectful to yourself and others through your actions, online and offline. And in doing this, a great question to ask yourself is, "What's the most loving, kind thing I can do?"

People that spread positivity and encouragement are magnetic! We need more of these kinds of people in this world, so join the party! Remember, what we put out in this world we are likely to receive. When we leave negative comments, we should expect to receive a lot of negativity back. In contrast, when we spread love and kindness in all that we do, we will receive blessings in return. It might sound cliché, but it's a fact. I've seen it happen time and time again.

DAILY CHALLENGE:

Before you leave a comment, make a post, or send a message, take a moment to make sure it is kind and respectful, and it reflects the kind of person you want to be. If you would not say it to the person's face, definitely don't message or post it! Once a comment or message is posted or sent, assume all your friends will see it. Evaluate your posts that way. Would you be cool with that? If the answer is yes, then you're good to go!

DAILY INSPIRATION:

Therefore, as God's chosen people, holy and dearly loved, clothe yourselves with compassion, kindness, humility, gentleness and patience. (Colossians 3:12 NIV)

CHAPTER 9

Never Give Up on Your Dreams

Never give up. Your breakthrough is coming!

If money didn't matter, what would you want to do with your life? What makes you come alive when you think about it? What can you do for hours and hours without realizing the time has passed? Call it our dreams, our passions, our calling, whatever you want to call it. I believe we all have something special that we've been put on this earth to do.

It is important that you courageously follow what God has put in your heart, and the passions He puts inside you. This doesn't mean they will necessarily be the same forever either; as you grow and develop, you'll discover new passions along the way. And they look different for each of us. Everyone's passions are just as important as another's, no matter how big or small they may seem.

But let me tell you, just saying this doesn't make it easy,

trust me! Social media might make it look easy, but any dream or passion worth pursuing is going to require work to get you there. The journey is going to be really tough, so at least pick something you love doing. No matter what you do, there is no "easy" path. Make sure you pick something that makes the challenge worth it!

When we live our lives like giving up is not an option, it's incredible how our dreams can become reality. Living committed is powerful. This doesn't mean committed for a day, or a week, or a month. Having a mindset of *never giving up* is being willing to spend years dedicated to our pursuits.

Instant gratification is a real problem present in our generation. We've grown up with getting information in milliseconds at the push of a button, thanks to technology. It's amazing and awesome, and we are so fortunate to have so much information available to us globally, but it has its dark side.

Because we are so used to instant gratification, we are not very patient if we have to wait. We want it all *now*. Surely you can all relate! We want the fruit, but we don't want to go through the slow and steady process of nurturing good soil, carefully planting the seeds, patiently watering and fertilizing to grow a healthy tree that will produce the quality of fruit we desire.

Imagine if you made a commitment to three years of going all-out to create your ideal life. What if you committed three years to being the best friend you could be, to staying present and connected with God, to being consistent every day with the small tasks that over time create a big success? What if you stayed faithful to your commitments, no matter how difficult it gets? Imagine what you could do and become!

If you are going through a difficult time right now and feel like giving up, remember that your perseverance through this struggle is preparing you for the blessings you will receive! *Diamonds start out as rough stones, and are brought into beauty from immense pressure and heat—creating and developing an incredible life is no different.* There will be pressure and struggle along the way. But be faithful to the journey. Once you put in the hard work and dedication through the challenges, you'll shine like no other ever could!

This is a reminder for me, just as it may be for you. I know how difficult it can be to stay the course. But I'll be real, literally every time in the past that I quit on a part of my life that was important to me, I look back and realize that I quit right before my breakthrough moment was coming. Every time I have given up on a passion of mine because it became difficult, I've regretted it. On the flip side, even if the end result didn't work out the way I had hoped or planned it would, I have never regretted sticking it through and following my God-given passions.

I do need to mention that sometimes, as we grow and mature, we discover our original plan or dream may not be what we actually want anymore. Rather, it has morphed into something else that fits more in line with where we feel God is leading us now. That will happen, as it has to me. But that's all a part of the fun and excitement of life! The important thing is, don't ever give up or lose hope in yourself and your dreams.

When you feel like quitting, remember, this may be the moment you are close to a breakthrough. Hang in there. *You just need to hang in there.* God has given you your passions for a reason. Stay faithful to those God-given passions, and even when you must make course corrections, never quit.

Never give up. Your breakthrough is coming!

DAILY CHALLENGE:

Do you feel like giving up on a passion God has placed inside your heart? If you do, stay on course! Don't give up! Pledge to either make a course correction, or keep heading forward. Write down your goals and pray for opportunities to grow and develop toward them. Be willing to put in the hard work required to see the amazing fruit of your labor, and be patient while that fruit grows. Watch for blessings ahead, and fully embrace them when they come!

DAILY INSPIRATION:

And let us run with endurance the race God has set before us. (Hebrews 12:1 NLT)

CHAPTER 10

Create More Than You Consume

Don't just watch the game of life happening around you, be an active player in it.

Some people say social media is a total waste of time. Aside from time wasted on content with no positive value, this isn't reflective of the truth when using certain social media in the right ways. Social media is an incredible tool, and it can be a great benefit to your life!

That being said, social media *can* become a waste of time when you just consume content all day long. Do you ever find yourself sitting on the couch, watching YouTube videos and browsing your Instagram feed, and then suddenly realize hours have gone by?

Browsing your feed for hours and hours can definitely be a waste of time! If you are anything like me, it's pretty tempting to want to spend lots of time surfing an endless supply of extremely entertaining or informative content. It's just so easy with the recommended videos and pictures these apps entice us with. You feel like you just *have to* watch one more tutorial video, one last prank, one more vlog, or one more _____ (fill in the blank!). Of course you don't "have to," but it definitely feels that way in the moment, doesn't it?

Time can really run away from me when I'm indulging in what I call "productive procrastination." (Yeah, you can laugh at the irony!) I'm productively procrastinating when I watch inspirational videos all day long. It's so ironic—I feel like I'm taking action on my dreams by watching videos about people telling me to take action on my dreams. *That's definitely not taking action*! It's not that the content is not valuable to me, it's just when it keeps me from doing the things I should be doing, it is not serving me anymore.

This form of procrastination is very sneaky. These videos are great and motivating, but at some point the phone needs to stop being a distraction, and we need to start moving forward in our goals. At the end of the day, you know deep down what you should be doing. You know the tasks you've been putting off that really need to get done, whether that be school projects, chores, new skills you want to learn, getting ahead at work, new relationships you want to build, and so on. I totally get it—sometimes it can just feel so difficult to actually get started on your own responsibilities with so much information bombarding you all the time at your fingertips.

I've learned some great ways to redeem my productive time that I'd like to share with you. When I catch myself procrastinating, here is what I do: I set a time limit. Yes, totally simple, but simple works. I'll give myself five minutes to watch the video, then I have to spend at least five minutes on productivity. After that, I'll set the timer for ten minutes of productivity and five minutes for watching videos. I'll continue raising the time for productivity (but keeping the shorter video time the same), going back and forth between work and entertainment until I get into a flow of working. Basically, I'm easing myself into productivity (since sometimes it's too difficult to just jump right in).

The good news is, once I'm in a flow, I can be productive for hours! That's the honest truth! It can just be difficult to get there. I encourage you to try this method out when you find yourself "productively procrastinating" online, or even better, experiment with your own methods for enhancing productivity!

Another productivity tip is to get the most difficult tasks done first thing when you wake up. To give an example, writing this book is not part of my typical schedule, and it can definitely feel overwhelming. So I've been waking up at 5:00 AM to write for a few hours every day before my normal schedule starts. Otherwise, I'm at risk for procrastinating on it, and writing quality content is very important to me. This works well, since I get it done first thing in the morning when my brain is refreshed. I definitely encourage you to try this with your extra projects or responsibilities.

Like I said before and will say again, social media is an amazing tool from which to learn, communicate, and reach out to others. But if we only use it to browse the feed for hours and hours, then it definitely will be a distraction from what is really important for us to do. Just be careful of that.

Make sure that you are spending more time *creating* than consuming content. And this doesn't just mean creating online, it means creating and developing yourself as a person as you live life with people. Set time limits on consumption if you need to. Don't just watch the game of life happening around you, be an active player in it!

DAILY CHALLENGE:

Entertainment is great, but set a time limit on your consumption, so you know you are not wasting valuable time to get your own work done and develop yourself. If you're having trouble putting the phone down, try setting a timer for five minutes on the phone, and then five minutes dedicated to productivity. Continue to increase the time dedicated to productivity until you get into a flow where productivity is the dominant task. The goal should always be to create more than you consume!

DAILY INSPIRATION:

Work brings profit, but mere talk leads to poverty! (Proverbs 14:23 NLT)

CHAPTER 11

Escape the Comparison Trap

Be inspired by other people's online victories, and
celebrate with them, but never compare their
highlights to your real life with all
its ups and downs.

"**W**hy don't I look like they do? Why can't I experience what they do? Why am I not as far
in my career as he is? Why can't I have
his/her life?"

Like I mentioned before, we've all experienced this at one
point or another, comparing ourselves to others. I call it the
"comparison trap," because you can't win—it's a trap. There
will always be someone that is more popular, better looking,
more talented, smarter, richer, the list goes on. Most of the
time, we compare and even draw false conclusions when we
don't know the full story.

Many lifestyles portrayed on social media are not what
they may appear. Trust me on this one. When we are scroll-

ing through our feed, we don't know how much they photoshopped the picture. We don't know if that's actually their car. The secret is out—almost nobody's life is what it looks like on social media. You'd be surprised how when the camera goes off, some people are completely different than how they came across online. It is no longer that perfect online life. They are no different than everybody else.

I get this question fairly often, "Justin, how are you so happy all the time?" "How are you always so smiley?" These questions always make me laugh, although I have to say I appreciate the kind words! They've just never seen me after my exam grade isn't what I wanted, or after too many sleepless nights, or after my computer keeps glitching up while I'm trying to get a song produced. Those situations have caused some serious frowns to say the least! So, if someone compares themselves to me being "happy all the time," that would be a false comparison! Do you get it?

Of course I'm stressed sometimes, I'm scared sometimes, and I wish I could do better most of the time. Maybe you can relate to that. I heard a pastor say one time that we need to stop sizing up details about our personal lives and its ups and downs with other people's selected online content. I really like that!

Almost every notable achievement by anyone comes with many failures and hardships. But most all of us don't post pictures during the hardships, so we only see the highlights. And honestly, that's okay. We can post what we want others to celebrate with us, and we can celebrate what others post with them. We just need to remember that the feed doesn't tell the full story (and privacy is important and okay).

Honestly, we all have the same fears and insecurities. If you are having anxiety over something, most likely the rest of us have experienced the same at some point. Even NBA basketball legend Kobe Bryant admitted struggling with insecurities from time to time. In an interview, he discussed how his feelings of self-doubt and fear of failure can creep in before a game, but when he embraces them and confronts them with the truth of who he is and what he is capable of, it helps him push toward his goals even more.

People are all the same, no matter how many followers they have! The insecurities and struggles that every human goes through doesn't change according to the number of followers, likes, or friends. God has put us all in a particular place in our journey for a reason. If you are not where you want to be, move forward in faith that you will get to where you need to go.

Focus your energy on the present. There is no need to compare where you are to someone else; you're not responsible to live their life, only your own. Be faithful to be the best you can be with what you've uniquely been given, treat the people God has put in your life with love and kindness, and don't fall for the comparison trap. That's how you win in life. Staying true to who God made you to be is the best way to live.

DAILY CHALLENGE:

Remember that people post their highlights on social media; they don't typically show the relatable struggles. So today, be inspired by other people's victories, and celebrate with them, but never compare their online highlights to your real life with all its ups and downs. You don't know the full story, and it does you no good to compare. Stay focused on your vision, and have faith in the unique journey that is ahead for you.

DAILY INSPIRATION:

Pay careful attention to your own work, for then you will get the satisfaction of a job well done, and you won't need to compare yourself to anyone else. (Galatians 6:4 NLT)

CHAPTER 12

Find Joy in the Process

There is serious joy to be found in working hard to reach your potential.

Before we dive in, I want to be clear that although worldly success does not define your worth as a person, I believe that there is serious joy to be found in working hard to reach your potential. Deep down in all of us, I believe there are unique God-given passions and dreams that we are wired to want to achieve. It's so important to follow your passion and work to make your dreams a reality.

That being said, when we work, we must work from a place of faith rather than desperation. We know that no matter what we achieve (and post about on social media), it doesn't make a difference to our worth as a person. Once we understand that, we can actually pursue our dreams in a fun way because we don't need to attach to any certain outcome. Does that make sense? Now that we understand that, let's jump into some encouragement for your ambitions and dreams.

When you surf your social media feed and see others succeed, sometimes it can come across like those successes came easy. I can certainly speak for myself to say that true success worth anything comes from hours of hard work and dedication. Every worthwhile achievement has come from a journey made up of small wins along the way. Every big success is made up of many small positive actions that *add up over time*. Good things take time. You may have heard that before, but it's worth repeating.

Fulfilling your passions takes time. We are blessed to live in a generation where we can find information and what we want almost instantly, but reaching for your dreams isn't one of them. Although it can look like it came easy for some people, it almost never does. Everyone goes through wins and losses, that's just a part of life. Find joy in the journey of life, not just in getting to the destination. In other words, see the process of reaching your dreams as important as achieving them in the end. It is all part of becoming the best you that you can be.

Personally, I'm a visionary, and I like to spend my time looking out and planning for the future. Sometimes it is difficult for me to just get moving with the first step in the present. Maybe you can relate to that sometimes? *The key is to just start.* Every accomplishment I've been proud of in my life came with a lot of perseverance and patience, including inevitable obstacles to overcome.

And I'll also mention, most of my successes took a long time to accomplish. I've never considered myself to be naturally talented at anything in particular, other than being able to focus and work really hard at what I want to achieve. Let me give you an example that would relate to social media—releasing music and content. It took me years to cultivate the skills I needed to write, record, produce, film, and edit as well as find people who wanted to listen.

I've been working at it since I was eleven, and it's only started to get attention from others in the past few years. I had to really fall in love with the small actions that led me to improve every day. Daily I would work on content, even when no one was watching. I would force myself to keep at my vocal exercises no matter how monotonous they seemed. I would learn from my mistakes and failures every day, and figure out ways to improve the next time around.

If I would have compared myself to others back then, I wasn't very good, but I was loving the creativity and the process of improving, so it didn't matter. Whatever is in your heart that you want to achieve, it can't be rushed. It will take time. I've seen this in my life, and every mentor of mine has told me the same exact thing is true in their lives as well.

If you are going to achieve great things, you also need to know that some tasks you'll have to do to get there won't be fun at first. But the more you do them, the better you'll get, and the more you'll enjoy doing those tasks.

For instance, hosting a livestream show was scary to me at first, and I wasn't good at it. I was super nervous. Even though you're talking to a camera, there are real people on the other side, and it's all real-time so there's no going back and editing the mess-ups. And I certainly messed up tons in the beginning. It took me awhile to let go and learn how to be engaging on camera. But once I did, it became so fun.

The reason I mention this is because I did not quit when I wasn't good at it. *I decided to commit to the process of learning, instead of judging myself for being inadequate.* I knew that cultivating the skill of hosting a livestream was needed to impact more people—a vision I felt God had put in my heart, so I kept at it. And after a few years of learning, my livestreams went from talking to myself, to engaging with over 130,000 people at one time tuned into my live show.

I want to encourage you that *all good things take time*. Don't give up when you are early in the journey and feel like success may be too far away. If you're working hard but feeling like you are not as far ahead as you wish you were, trust me, you are way farther ahead than you think! And that breakthrough moment is coming. And when it comes, it is going to feel amazing, because you have put the effort in to make it happen!

Whatever vision God has given you, find satisfaction in the work it takes to get there. All you have is this present moment. So plan for the future, but don't get caught up in it. Instead, focus your energy on having fun and working hard in this moment right now. Learn to enjoy the journey of life rather than living only for the end destination. Let's make every moment count!

DAILY CHALLENGE:

Whatever your goal is, write down three ways that you could increase your skills needed to achieve it, including having fun while making progress toward that goal. You're training yourself to actually enjoy working toward something you know will be worth all the dedication put into getting there. Even if the work doesn't seem inherently exciting, get creative and find ways to make it fun! There's fun to be had in everything, and knowing you are working toward your dream will give you joy along the journey, as you embrace each moment of it.

DAILY INSPIRATION:

Lazy people want much but get little, but those who work hard will prosper. (Proverbs 13:4 NLT)

CHAPTER 13

How Would This Read on Headline News?

Walk your talk — then when all eyes are on you, you've got nothing to hide.

Is there really any privacy anymore on social media? For better or worse, no, not really. We already talked about how there are real consequences when it comes to what we post, but I thought it would be important to further address privacy. For some reason, I feel like our generation doesn't fully understand the importance of this, because I've seen this issue cause so many problems.

In my experience, nothing is private anymore when it comes to social media. Those "private" messages you think you're sending aren't actually private. And let me add, never believe anyone who says they won't share the message. Always assume they will, because anything can be shared, accidentally even. I've seen so many unnecessary problems arise from a few private messages broadcasted to others. Once a message is sent, it can be easily screenshot, stored, and traced back to the original sender.

I've heard many horror stories from people I know who got into lots of trouble from a couple of irresponsible messages or social media posts. Not only can relationships be ruined, but even future career opportunities. Trust me when I say that every scholarship donor, future employer or potential business partner will stalk your social media feed. At my friend's company, they make hiring decisions sometimes based on how the candidates represent themselves on social media.

What can we learn from this? Just *always assume publicity.* Assume your messages or posts will get shared, even if the recipient promises they won't show anyone. Before sending a message, imagine it blasted out to all your friends and family. Better yet, imagine it on headline news! If that thought makes you nauseous, don't hit send. I'm half kidding, but honestly, do whatever it takes to make sure you protect yourself from sending anything that could harm you or others in the long run, or even close the door on opportunities for you in the future.

There is a real peace that comes from aligning your actions with your beliefs and values (basically, not doing stupid stuff you know you shouldn't and then regretting it later). Becoming a confident, happy person means owning what you say and do. Being proud of the choices you make. None of us are perfect. I'm far from it. But that doesn't mean we shouldn't aim to be the best human we can possibly be.

I'd like to add one more point to this which I think is really important, and although I dive into it more in other chapters, I want to touch on it quickly. You have so much potential! I seriously believe that you can achieve so much more than you could ever imagine—so dream big! Dream crazy, big dreams because you seriously can achieve them.

Here's the thing though: When you start really playing the game at a pro level, you're going to be in the public eye. Guess what happens when you're in the public eye? If you have any hidden spiders, they'll all come creeping out.

We see this happening in the news everywhere. Celebrities and politicians are paying the consequences of mistakes they made years ago. It may not always seem fair, especially if the people have turned their lives around, but it's the way it works. And it's not that they cannot bounce back from that, but unfortunately, some really never completely do. I just wanted to add this in to really encourage you to believe in yourself by posting and messaging what you're proud of, and what you'll remain proud of for the long haul. Don't post or message anything you wouldn't want blasted out on a billboard.

Always hold to this value: *Walk your talk—so that when all eyes are on you, you've got nothing to hide.* That is confident, purposeful living, and what you deserve to experience!

Our lack of privacy doesn't have to be a bad thing. It just means we need to hold ourselves to a higher standard. Then, when people talk about what we're doing, it just affirms our character. It feels really good to live that way anyway, don't you think? And remember, when we act from encouragement and love, online and offline, we have nothing to worry about!

DAILY CHALLENGE:

As extreme as this may sound, before you post or message

something online, especially if you're second-guessing whether you should send or post it or not, imagine it being up on a billboard (because I believe you may be in a position of influence where that really could happen one day!). If you don't feel comfortable with that thought, I encourage you to re-think what you're about to message or post. If it passes that test, and it is in line with your values, then go for it!

DAILY INSPIRATION:

Let everything you say be good and helpful, so that your words will be an encouragement to those who hear them. (Ephesians 4:29 NLT)

CHAPTER 14

Take a Break!

Unplugging from social media re-connects you to who you are without it — that's important to staying true to the real you.

I don't know about you, but when I enjoy something, I want to spend all my time doing it! And since social media offers so many different and fun things to watch, create, edit, post, etc., I'm tempted to never want to put the phone down. What are healthy limits when it comes to social media?

Being overly obsessed with social media is a very real thing—checking notifications first thing in the morning, continuing all throughout the day, and browsing the feed before going to sleep. Anyone else do this sometimes? I definitely have. Social media is saturated with an endless amount of content, which is great for our entertainment, but it can consume *way* too much of our time (and our lives for that matter!). I've definitely fallen into social media obsession at times, and I doubt you have escaped it either!

In my experience, the best way to snap out of being obsessed with the newsfeed is to *take a break*! Breaks are a must! If you ever start feeling totally consumed with social media, my best advice is to go MIA (Missing In Action) for a few days, or even a few weeks. Just turn all notifications off, or turn your phone off, and focus on something completely different. How crazy would that be? If you can't bear the thought of leaving your phone for the day (or if your heart is beating fast as you read this), I think it's time to take a break!

This is so important, because what we take into our minds from our phone shapes who we become. Knowledge and information (including entertainment) shape us, whether we want to admit it or not. Have you ever heard the saying, "what goes in must come out?" Or "garbage in, garbage out?" The former president of Facebook recently shared publicly that social media is now harming society relationally and productivity-wise, and he is even worried about children's brains. (*Ouch!*) That's the former president of Facebook— what does he know that we don't?

We shouldn't allow ourselves to be passively influenced and shaped by others—what we expose ourselves to online molds us. So I encourage you to not be passive with it! While browsing content, ask yourself, "Is this helping me become the person I want to be?" And don't let your phone be the only thing that shapes you—there's so much more to life than online content consumption!

A couple of years ago, I became too obsessed with social media. Notifications were always on my mind. I was constantly on my phone, and I was missing real experiences. During that time, I had an opportunity to live on a boat for a week and just unplug from everything. No wifi, no cell reception. I know, crazy right?! I remember thinking, "Oh no, if I leave for a week, everyone will forget about me!" Seems ridiculous, but I'm sure you get what I'm talking about!

Thankfully, I went on the trip. It was amazing, and it felt so refreshing to unplug. I was able to come back with a clear head and a new perspective, and it saved me from an eventual burn-out.

Unplugging from social media re-connects you to who you are without it—that's important to staying true to the real you. Social media doesn't define you! It's literally just a bunch of apps that could be here today and gone tomorrow. Just learning to be unplugged, to think and reflect, without a firehose of data streaming at you, will make you a better you.

I encourage you to take a break from the phone every once in awhile, especially when you start feeling anxious from it. Instead, do something unique that you normally don't do, and change up your routine. It doesn't have to be as extreme as living on a boat, but just try something different.

Go for a run or a long walk if you don't normally exercise, try out a new hobby, leave your phone at home for a day... it can be anything. Just make sure you are away from the online world. I promise, everyone will still be there when you come back, and you'll come back with more of the real you to offer! This world has so many beautiful experiences to be lived and enjoyed, and if you are constantly on your phone, *you will miss them.*

DAILY CHALLENGE:

Give yourself a break! Plan a day to leave your phone several hours (or the entire day) and go do something you will fully enjoy without constant distraction. If you can't imagine a day without your phone, then I challenge you to take a longer break! However long you need to feel refreshed. Break your routine and do something new you have never tried before, or something you have been wishing you had time to experience or have been missing being able to do.

DAILY INSPIRATION:

Then Jesus said, "Come to me, all of you who are weary and carry heavy burdens, and I will give you rest. Take my yoke upon you. Let me teach you, because I am humble and gentle at heart, and you will find rest for your souls." (Matthew 11:28,29 NLT)

CHAPTER 15

Celebrate Other People's Successes

Trade out comparison and competition for celebration and collaboration.

L et me tell you, nothing will hold you back more from staying true to who God made you to be than feeling jealous and inferior to other people. As I mentioned in the first chapter, when we browse our social media feed, we so often ask ourselves questions like, "Why didn't I get the grade that she did?" "It's not fair that I work harder, and they are farther ahead than I am!" "Why don't I have a girlfriend like he does?" "Why does she get noticed and not me, when I deserve it more?" "How come I'm not starting on the team like he is?" ...and on and on and on.

One story really sticks out to me in my own life that I want to share with you. I remember the first time I was pitched to a record label my senior year of high school. I wanted it so badly! I worked so hard, sacrificed other important things to prepare for it, and really felt like God was opening the door. But, they picked up another artist over me. That really hit me hard and clouded up my mind for a few months. I remember feeling so jealous, scrolling through the list of the label's artists and wishing I was there too.

In my opinion, nothing kills confidence more than jealousy. Jealousy will lead you on a path far from your true self. It lies to you, telling you that your worth or value is relative— relative to how you compare. But that's not the truth, nor is it reality! *Jealousy will lock you in a prison of comparison, holding you back from reaching your full potential and being true to the best version of you.*

Even though it used to attack my mind, I'm very happy to say that I almost never feel jealous anymore! I've trained my mind to replace those immediate jealous thoughts with thoughts of praise for the other person. It took a long time, but that positive habit *can* be formed.

Because here's the thing, we aren't in competition with each other. We would all be 100 times happier if we could free ourselves from feeling like we have to compete with each other! Competition of this type creates an illusion of separateness and scarcity. Truth is, this world is abundant with resources. *We can all win.* Let me repeat that, we can all win! If you succeed at something, I can succeed too, and vice versa.

When I scroll through my feed and see success stories, instead of feeling jealousy kick in, I've trained myself to immediately catch those jealous thoughts and replace them with feelings of *inspiration*. In fact, my aim is to feel inspired and energized when I see others winning. Instead of feeling jealous and inferior of other people's successes, I think of ways to build them up (just like I'd want if I had a win) and build with them. I put my energy toward thinking of ways we can build and grow together! As you can imagine, this is a totally different mindset. Trade out *comparison* and *competition* for *celebration* and *collaboration.*

To make it practical, when you look at your feed and see others succeed, be happy for them. Their personal victories are separate from yours, so you can come alongside them and celebrate with them. Just because other people experience success doesn't mean it will affect your potential for it! Be inspired to know that if they can do it, you can too. Then think of ways to learn from their success or collaborate with them if your interests are like-minded.

Unlike ever before, we have an abundance of resources at our fingertips. Earth's population is over 7.4 billion, and the global currencies' total is well over 80 trillion! That's definitely more than enough for everyone. I have to remind myself every day to not fall into the trap of comparison and the jealousy and inferiority that stems from it. Jealousy is a danger to you—it's toxic. Avoid it like it's the poison that it is.

Let me add one last point. This world worships material success, but it should never be what is most important to you. You can't take it with you. Experiences and relationships beat material objects any day. What truly matters is how you treat others. Are you loving those around you?

You don't have to worry about comparing or competing with others. You don't have to worry about flexing more than your friends on social media. The only thing you need to "worry" about is that your heart is in the right place. If you're going to worry about anything, worry that you would love those around you better.

DAILY CHALLENGE:

If you are scrolling your feed, and you see successes from others that might initially spark jealousy, instead, congratulate the people and validate them in a way that will build them up. As you do this, let it inspire you to continue to embrace your own journey, knowing there are blessings specifically for you coming too. Think about collaborating rather than competing. If others are like-minded and would be fun to collaborate with, reach out to join them in the journey, or seek ways to learn from them. Trade out comparison and competition for celebration and collaboration!

DAILY INSPIRATION:

Love is patient, love is kind. Love is not jealous or boastful or proud. (1 Corinthians 13:4 NLT)

CHAPTER 16

Stay True to You

God made you unique, and that uniqueness is what needs to be shared with the world.

How easy is it to fake a persona on social media? *Too easy!* Let me explain. One of my friends interned and wrote some really cool blogs for an online magazine—you might know the magazine's name. She is such a talented writer. Several years later, the magazine started stealing her work and publishing it under their own writers' names. The magazine's "writers" who were stealing my friend's work had very active and engaged profiles, with tons of followers and activity on their pages.

Come to find out, they were all fake accounts created by the magazine. The writers' personas were totally faked. The magazine's management had created the popular writers' accounts using other girls' pictures found online. How creepy is that?!

My guess as to why they did this was to make it look as though their magazine had very popular writers. But they would completely plagiarize and steal content from young talented writers to post as their own. This seriously happened. What's crazy is the accounts had been active for years, so they had been faking everyone out for who knows how long!

When I heard that happened, it blew my mind. Who would have imagined that? I wonder how many other fake accounts are out there? I wonder how many "perfect" personas I've been comparing myself to have been fake? Either faking a lifestyle (fancy cars, expensive clothes, vacations, etc.), or in this magazine's case, literally faking everything. You never know the full story.

We are in desperate need of authenticity and integrity on social media. We need to be people who are confident enough in our authenticity, that there is no need to make things up that aren't true. We need people who aren't afraid to be real and relatable. If I'm honest, I used to feel like I had to be perfect. I couldn't post a picture unless it was perfect quality, perfect this, or perfect that. I couldn't upload a new song unless everything was perfect. I heard in my head, "No one will like me if it's not perfect!" This belief led to so much frustration because I always came up short.

What is "perfect" anyway? Who knows. Relative standards like this can really do damage to us. Since "perfect" is really subjective, and there is no true definition, we will stress ourselves out trying to attain it—whatever "it" is. But this belief I held caused a lot of stress and insecurity in my life back then. Truth is, when I tried to be perfect and never show a fault to get approval from others, it actually turned people away from me. No one liked the "trying-so-hard-to-be-perfect" Justin, and neither did I because it wasn't real. *No one likes perfect, cause none of us are.* When someone tries to create that perfect facade, we can all see through it.

If you want people to genuinely like you, *just be you*. Simple as that! If you haven't heard this recently—who you are is incredible! No one else is like you. You're the 100% original, authentic and genuine YOU. God created you unique for a reason. You don't ever need to put on a persona to be "liked." When you're being authentic, you're going to attract the right kind of people in your life. And the truth is, you're never really going to feel truly loved by a community of people unless you feel good enough about yourself to show them the real you.

Your uniqueness is what needs to be shared with the world. You were created as a one-of-a-kind Masterpiece—a work of art. Only God knows your true value and worth, and that's why you need to own who you are. No one else on earth can be or do what you were uniquely created to be and do!

Of course, everyone has an opinion, and some people won't like what you're doing. This is especially true in our Internet generation, where billions of people all over the world are at your fingertips, so that is a lot of opinions! Given this, you've got to just realize that there will always be those that don't appreciate you like they should, or that undervalue you, and that goes for every one of us.

And you know what? That's okay. We don't have to please everybody! There are so many people in this world; the ones who resonate with you will find you, and you'll find them. We are all works of art in process—no one's finished yet. People enjoy seeing the progress (even if there are a few mess-ups along the way), so always keep it real. Authenticity always wins in the end. Share the real you in your real story.

DAILY CHALLENGE:

Today, be authentic to the true you. Your uniqueness, even your quirkiness and dorkiness, is what makes you amazing. There is no such thing as "cool" anyway. No one wants perfect, so don't feel like you have to be. When you post on social media, post the real you. Of course, put your best out there, but make sure it is authentic to your beliefs and values. You'll attract true friends that you will actually enjoy!

DAILY INSPIRATION:

For we are God's masterpiece. He has created us anew in Christ Jesus, so we can do the good things he planned for us long ago. (Ephesians 2:10 NLT)

CHAPTER 17

Alone on Friday Night

It's so easy to surround-sound your life with noise, people and screens and never get comfortable just being alone with yourself.

It's a Friday afternoon. My mind is racing. "What am I going to do tonight?! No one has texted me back... But it's the weekend. I HAVE to do something. Otherwise... everyone's going to think I'm a loner... Even worse—I'll think I'm a loner."

That was me a while ago. I couldn't stand being alone. And if I ever found myself in that position, I would just distract myself with entertaining videos on YouTube. The problem was that I would spend all my time trying to have a bunch of friends and feel popular, but I never took the time to get to know me. That sounds pretty funny—"get to know me." It's true, though. I had made myself so busy that I lost touch with who I was deep down—with my authentic self, and my dreams and goals that came with it.

This generation basically promotes being distracted 24/7,

sometimes even dangerously. People try excessive partying or drinking or drugs or Netflix binges or social media addictions or everything in between—it's just so easy to surround-sound your life with noise and people and screens, and never get comfortable just being alone with yourself.

Don't ever be afraid to be alone. That's when you find out more about who you really are and the message you want to share through your life. Because the truth is, I can say "stay true to you" all day long, but if you aren't clear on *who you actually are*, that doesn't help at all.

I have to admit, for the longest time the "be yourself" advice you hear everywhere you go never helped me much. I relate to it way more now that I have a clear sense of who I am, but for the majority of high school, I wasn't clear on who I wanted to be. I filled my schedule so full that I was "too busy" to be alone. To be real with you, I was deeply scared of being alone. I never realized that alone time didn't mean I was lonely. In fact, making time to be alone was the best thing I could have done to *not* feel lonely.

Confusing? Well, it's because it's so counter to what we are programmed to do. The more you learn to be alone and quiet with your own thoughts, the more you know you, and who you want to be. The more confidently you know yourself, the more confident you feel with others and their diversity. Soon, you don't need others to feel good about yourself, so being alone doesn't make you feel lonely!

Now, I literally schedule out time in my day to just be alone and write what comes to mind, so I can stay in touch daily with myself, my goals, and where I feel God is leading me to next. I turn the phone off. I get outside in nature with a pen and paper, and I realign with who I am and what I feel I was put on this earth to do. I pray for friends and family, and ask God for guidance. It's amazing how much more centered and confident I feel when I make time to do this. And I realize... I'm never really alone!

I can't tell you who you are deep down, or what you feel your deepest passions and dreams are, only you can discover that. But I can encourage you to make time for that discovery. God speaks to your heart when you make non-distracted time to listen. *Alone time doesn't mean you're lonely.* If you haven't experienced this yet, it might be the most important thing you could do to accomplish your God-given potential.

DAILY CHALLENGE:

Get your calendar out and schedule some time this week to be alone with God, focusing on your passions and dreams, and the person you want to become. Listen for promptings and guidance, and write things down as they come to your mind. Gather ideas that will keep you staying true to the best version of you.

DAILY INSPIRATION:

Guard your heart above all else, for it determines the course of your life. (Proverbs 4:23 NLT)

When Friends Let You Down

True friendship will have conflict sometimes — it is inevitable — so be committed to working things out in person, before letting any hurt begin to seed resentment in you.

We've already addressed that when we start authentically sharing content on social media, we are likely going to get people that don't like what we're about. As cliché as it is, "haters are gonna hate." When those haters are random people, it's an easy fix, just block them. But what about when we get negativity from a *friend*? What about when someone we love and care about is being really hurtful? We can't just block them if we are going to see them at school or work the next day...

Over the years, I've experienced some friends saying degrading things about me behind my back, offline and online. But I have to admit too, that when I was younger, I also have said things to friends and loved ones that I later regretted.

I'm sure you may have also sent messages or comments in the past that you would never have said to the person directly.

Social media can give a false sense of reality—a dangerous one at that. People easily say things that treat others like they have no feelings. And this goes for everyone! Just because someone is "famous" or has a large following doesn't mean they can't be hurt by cruel words too. It's as if people lose touch with their humanity, forgetting that there are *real people* with *real feelings* on the other end of the comment.

For whatever reason, people tend to say things on social media that they would never say in public. I am sure you have experienced people who are nice in person, but who can be completely different online. Sometimes, they actually might not even realize how they are coming across in the comment, message, or text, and may not have meant it in a hurtful way.

If a friend is being rude on one of your posts, my advice is to delete the comment and call them or text them in a new *private* conversation. This protects you and your friend from having your personal issue being broadcasted for everyone to read, and the important thing anyway is that you work things out with them.

Really resist the temptation to comment back to them in the comment stream. I've seen friends get in fights in the comments and it rarely does any good, instead it makes everything really awkward. If the comment was hurtful, delete the comment, then text them for a time to call or meet up. Always try to work it out in person if you can. Our relationships are so important.

So much of our interaction is nonverbal when we talk in person, so it is very easy to misread online communication.

This seems crazy, but in researching, I found that *over half* of communication is body language! And if that isn't surprising enough, more than a third is the *tone* of your voice, and get this: *less than a tenth* of communication is the actual words you say. That means texts and DMs require us to actually *guess* at over 90 percent of what we can pick up in a face-to-face conversation!

It can just be so difficult to read how the other person is feeling through a comment or text, and many times we immediately jump to the *worst* case scenario, which is most likely not the *true* case scenario. It's always best to have the mindset of giving people the benefit of the doubt first, and then reach out to clear things up if things were worse than you expected.

So, how do you do this? Crucial conversations should always be in person if at all possible, and if you are not in the same location, video call is the next best thing. If that can't happen, then a phone call. Just don't do it over DMs or texts!

Another helpful tip is to always go into the conversation *expecting the best* (our natural bias is to assume the worst, but it just makes things worse!). Even if going into the conversation makes you nervous, still do your best to give your friends the benefit of the doubt, and assume that they will be happy to work things out.

It's almost funny how difficult text communication is to read accurately. I'll share an example in high school when one of my closest friends seemed to ghost me for a week. He'd either read my text and not reply, or he would send back a super short answer. My mind was racing with questions like, "What did I do?!" "Are we not friends anymore?" I finally met up with him at the end of the week. Come to find out, he had the busiest week ever! Relatives were in town, intense work week, big school projects due, his girlfriend came to visit from out of state—just one of those weeks. He wasn't mad at me at all, just busy. I totally read the situation wrong. Goes to show how important in-person communication is!

Most often our friends don't intend to hurt us, but sadly sometimes they will. Just like you or I might unintentionally hurt one of our friends. Regardless, always try to restore the friendship in person rather than text and DMs. I totally get that this is hard to do. Dealing with conflict in person is nerve-racking. Your friends will probably be nervous too, but when you go in person, truly wanting to work things out, it will help them actually open up and be less defensive. In the next chapter, I will go into more detail about having these conversations.

If for whatever reason they don't want to make amends (I've been there), forgive them. But if their behavior doesn't change towards you, don't continue spending time with them. *Forgiveness shouldn't be confused with passivity.* We can forgive those who hurt us without ever hanging out with them again, especially if it's not healthy for our well-being.

I remember several years back, I heard that a friend of mine was saying pretty hurtful comments about my character to other mutual friends. At first I thought it was just gossip, which as you know is often not even true, but since I kept hearing about it, it really started to bother me. My first inclination was to send an angry text and call the friendship off. (I hadn't learned a lot of the lessons I have now!)

But I am so thankful I didn't send that text! I asked to meet in person instead. So we linked up and we were able to work it out. He had said some things, but they weren't nearly as bad as the way they were portrayed to me, and they were motivated by some hurt he had been feeling that I was able to apologize for. We both were able to apologize for ways we had hurt each other, all which came through misunderstandings. What's so awesome is we became so much closer after that day! That day, we created such a strong friendship because we had the maturity to drop our egos, apologize, and work things out.

Most people are good-hearted and have a lot of love to give, yet, still some people won't change from their hurtful ways and are set on dragging you down. Don't hang out with those people! God has put you here for a purpose and to be a blessing in this world, and it's so important to surround yourself with people who will encourage you to live out that purpose.

I have to say that I have found some truly incredible friends, both offline and online. I am confident you will be able to find them too. True friendship will have conflict sometimes—it is inevitable—so be committed to working things out in person before letting any hurt begin to seed resentment in you. God works in huge ways when we go the extra mile to mend relationships with others, and often addressing and resolving the conflict will strengthen the bonds of friendship even more!

DAILY CHALLENGE:

Commit today that from this point on, when you get a hurtful comment or message from a friend, you will send your friend a text to find a time to meet in person. (Maybe it's something you need to do today!) Always go into the conversation expecting the very best. Genuinely desire to work things out with your friend. Be real and tell them how you honestly feel, doing your best to not blame or accuse. If for whatever reason they don't want to make it right, forgive them in your heart, but don't feel like you have to continue spending any more time with them. Negativity will only distract you from achieving what God put you in this world to do.

DAILY INSPIRATION:

If it is possible, as far as it depends on you, live at peace with everyone. (Romans 12:18 NIV)

CHAPTER 19

Critical Conversations

A big part of cultivating great relationships is knowing how to deal with conflict in a healthy way.

Having great relationships with others is a critical component to a happy life. A big part of cultivating great relationships is knowing how to deal with conflict in a healthy way. Conflict is bound to happen at some point, no matter how great your relationships are now.

With almost everyone in our generation communicating digitally, it seems like effective conflict resolution has become a lost art. No doubt, it's difficult to live with happiness and confidence when you're stuck in the middle of a conflict or unnecessary drama. All that to say, knowing how to resolve conflict in your relationships is critical. As I mentioned in the previous chapter, I want to go into more detail on these critical in-person conversations in this chapter.

Resolving relational conflicts through text or DMs should always be a last resort, never a first choice. If I'm being real, social media, as amazing as it is, can be a crutch to avoid face-to-face interactions, especially when they are crucial conversations with important potential outcomes.

Conversations of importance should always be in person (or video call if you live apart). As I mentioned in the previous chapter, most of communication is nonverbal, so messaging important conversations can really mess things up. Basically, it's not just *what* we say, it's *how* we say it. Facial expressions, tone of voice, body language...they're all just as important as the words being said. This is why texts or DMs can create so much unnecessary conflict, because things are often misunderstood.

Trust me on this one. Growing up, I've made many mistakes texting what should have been said in person. I never meant for the text to be interpreted a certain way, but all the person had to go off of were the words they were reading. It was my fault. Even if in my head I was speaking with empathy, I should have known that literally no one can read empathy in a text! 90 percent of the communication had been cut off; all they had were the words.

When it comes to conflict, always, always, *always* try to resolve it in person first. I get it, it can be scary, but if you truly want to work the situation out, have the courage to meet up with the person. If that doesn't work, then call them. My point is, avoid texting when you need to resolve conflict. That way, you're able to communicate your heart 100 percent.

More than just conflicts, *all* important conversations should be in person, or as close to that as possible. I'll share with you a really embarrassing story having to do with a girl I really liked freshman year of high school. I remember, I really liked this girl, but I had no idea how she felt about me. I was super shy at the time, so I decided to text all her friends and ask how she felt about me (what could possibly go wrong with that idea!? *Everything!*) Definitely wasn't one of my best ideas... But the thought of talking to her face-to-face was nerve racking. I finally mustered up enough confidence to text the girl about how I felt. Oh great... Another very bad idea. I should never have texted that. As you might have guessed, it didn't work out with her.

She and her friends were totally put off by the fact that I didn't just talk in person. I'm literally laughing thinking back to this! (Oh, the funny things we do growing up!) After that, I remember vowing to myself to never text important conversations—especially when it involved a girl I was crushing on (ha!).

Trust me on this one. *Save your crucial conversations to resolve in person.* I just see so many people creating unnecessary problems by texting what should be face-to-face. Not only do face-to-face conversations resolve conflicts, but they will also build your confidence. Basically, the more personal, the better—text as a last resort only. And with friendships online, skype calls work great for this.

DAILY CHALLENGE:

Think about who you might need to have a crucial conversation with in order to keep your friendship strong. It may be a conflict to work through, or even misunderstanding to clear up. Commit to meeting up in person to talk, or video call if you don't live nearby. Don't let yourself settle for texting or messaging to work it out! Reach out to this person, always go in assuming the very best, and you'll find the conversation will most often lead to a positive outcome and a stronger friendship.

DAILY INSPIRATION:

"If your brother or sister [wrongs you], go and point out their fault just between the two of you. If they listen to you, you have won them over. (Matthew 18:15 NLT)

CHAPTER 20

Are You Ready for Your Blessings?

No more talking, it's time to start walking!

I heard a song browsing Soundcloud a few years ago, and it has stuck with me ever since. The lyric basically said something along the lines of, *"Are you ready for your blessings?"*

This song really spoke to me when I first heard it. It really had me thinking...was I preparing in the present for my ideal future? Was I planting seeds that could one day blossom into incredible opportunities? These questions really challenged me (and they continue to challenge me!). I had all these dreams, but was I living in faith that they were actually going to come true? I have to admit, at the time I really wasn't. I didn't fully believe in what God could do through me. I didn't fully commit to making my dreams a reality.

Because let's be real, talking about your dreams and goals is easy. Anyone can do that. But how many people actually *walk out* what they *talk out*? Very few. If I'm honest, I went through a period in my life where I was just a lot of talk. I would tell everyone about my future goals and visions like I was putting in work, yet looking back, a lot of the time I was on the couch watching YouTube videos of others living out their dreams.

The longer this went on, my confidence began to dwindle away. I wasn't experiencing joy throughout the day. Honestly, I was slipping into becoming lazy and complacent, and those who know me well know that this goes against the core of who I am, and just feels awful to me.

Basically, there are people who *want* something to happen, people who *hope* something will happen, and then there are those who actually *do* something in order to *make* it happen! Thankfully, I decided to start making it happen! I had to starting walking the talk again. I had to snap out of the rut, grow up, and start doing what I said I was going to do.

"No more *talking*, it's time to start *walking*," I told myself. I began to realize that every moment matters. Yes, right now. I believe God gives us the passions, but we have to take action to make them happen. And that means every small action that you do matters in the big picture.

How would you be acting if you were already living your dreams right now? How would you be feeling? What would you be doing? What are your ideal values you live by when you're living out your ideal life? What is stopping you from being that person today?

I love questions like these! We must realize that nothing has to stop us from being the person we want to be! We are blessed with a new start every day. Our thoughts dictate our actions, which dictate our reality. It starts with belief, but that belief is nothing without backing it up with action.

Now let me add a quick point. Use common sense on this one. I believe it is always best to build from your natural strengths. When I was younger, I enjoyed playing basketball and was a good player on my team, but putting all my time into trying to play pro basketball is obviously not what I was created for. I don't naturally excel at basketball, I don't have the height or the hops (that's why I transitioned to soccer!). God gave me this body for a reason, but it definitely wasn't meant for pro basketball.

It is very important to find things that you love, and that you are naturally good at. In my opinion, those come from God, and those passions need to be pursued. That doesn't mean that these gifts won't still need to be developed, and sometimes the passions we first think we were created to do lead us to our real purpose and passion.

An interesting story to illustrate this is about Michael Jordan. Believe it or not, his first dream was not to be a professional basketball player, it was actually to be a professional baseball player! He was once asked what it felt like to have fulfilled all of his dreams, since he was the most successful NBA basketball player ever in history. He shared that it wasn't until he let go of his dream playing baseball, and realized that he was built to play basketball, that he was able to achieve so much. Amazing!

There is nothing stopping you from acting like your ideal self today. Once you find what you love, and what you naturally excel at, your potential is literally limitless. Walk the talk! Start putting in the work to become amazing at what you love! Your confidence will sky-rocket, and you'll find a real joy that comes from working at something you find value in and love doing.

Every world-changing achievement has started with a

simple belief in the dream. Before anything else, it takes belief to turn a vision into reality. Whatever your vision is, believe that it will become reality. But most importantly, start *acting* like it will become a reality.

So, let me ask you: *Are you ready for your blessings?* They're on their way, so no more talking—it's time to start walking!

DAILY CHALLENGE:

Today, remind yourself that each minute matters. Begin planting seeds that will one day blossom into incredible future opportunities. God has created you with endless potential and possibilities—start living that way! Live like your dreams will come true. Hold yourself accountable for the little things. Always ask yourself before you act, "Will this benefit or hurt the future vision God has for my life?" And definitely, get ready for your blessings!

DAILY INSPIRATION:

"For I know the plans I have for you," says the Lord. "They are plans for good and not for disaster, to give you a future and a hope." (Jeremiah 29:11 NLT)

CHAPTER 21

Free Yourself from the Opinions of Others

It doesn't matter what other people say or do; nothing can change the truth about how special you are.

ver been worried about what other people think? That's a pretty silly question. We all have! And that's totally okay, I get it. It's not wrong to want others to like what we do. We just need to keep it in perspective.

For instance, I want you to like this book, but I have to be okay with the fact that some people who read it won't like it. I can't let the fear of whether you will like or dislike my book keep me from actually writing and releasing it. I have to remind myself that at the end of the day, some will love it and some won't, but as long as I believe in the message of the book, I need to release it regardless of what other people think.

We all struggle with what people think of us, but it gets

dangerous when we become *obsessed* with the opinions of others. This is especially true when we base our worth as a person on what other people think, or when we make big decisions based solely on the opinions of others.

Keep in mind, those who judge you are probably not your favorite people anyway, nor are they the ones who should be closest to you in your life. There are over seven billion people on this planet. If some people don't vibe with you, there are plenty of others out there who will!

But I totally understand, saying this is a lot easier than actually doing it. It's easier for me to write that we should "be free from other people's opinions," but it's way more difficult to actually live this out, *especially* with this social media-driven world we live in.

No doubt, we can probably all agree that social media has made it increasingly more difficult to free ourselves from what other people think of us. Because now, it's all about the likes and the follows. Like I mentioned earlier, at times I've felt like a part of my self-worth was directly related to the amount of likes I got. Typing that out seems ridiculous, but it's true. I would bet you can relate to that to a degree.

It's crazy to think how something as simple as likes on a post can have such an impact on our emotions. Even though I've always known I shouldn't base my worth on other people's opinions, I feel like I can honestly say that I have finally reached the point of being free of this, and I want you to be free too.

Sure, we all want people to like us, to think we're cool (still don't know what that means), smart, funny, and the list goes on. The fact of the matter is, being likeable, cool, smart, funny, etc., changes with the billions of opinions out there. To please everyone, you basically have to be a chameleon, adapting to whomever you are with at the time, and that is no fun at all. The happiest way to live is to be *you*, no more, no less.

For instance, unlike most of my friends, video games were never a big deal for me. In fact, I didn't grow up with a gaming system, I never liked playing them much, and I always felt like I'd rather be doing something else, like reading a book. I love to read. My friends would always joke around with me about that. Some people think that is really nerdy, but hey, it's me.

I also rescue bugs! Yes, even ants. It sounds crazy to most, but in my opinion, why not put them back in their habitat? So, my roommates at college had to put up with me trapping bugs and letting them out the window to go free if we saw one in the apartment. Funny thing is, after awhile, they even felt better scooting the bugs out the window instead of swatting them! Saving bugs is totally weird and dorky, but hey it's me. All that to say, it is best to just be who you are, nerdy or not!

And honestly, it feels great to just be myself, knowing I'm exactly the way God wired me. Once I finally gave up on stressing over others' opinions, and just owned my own unique personality, I can't even tell you how freeing that was! And to be honest, much of the time, the opinions of others weren't even what I thought anyway.

I'll share with you what has really helped me actually live this principle out over the past few years. The best thing I've done for my mental well-being is *finding my worth in the way God views me, not the way I think people view me.*

This has been a life changer for me. As I've said in previous chapters, I believe that God created you and me unique for a reason. My appearance and all its flaws were created for a reason. My personality and all the dorkiness that comes with it was created for a reason. The same is true for you! God created you unique and sees you as His amazing work of art, His treasure. You can let go of your insecurities.

Your personality, your appearance, your dreams and passions—*everything about you was created for a reason!* Understanding this can really free you to start living authentically. You see, once I gave up on "trying to be cool" to other people, I found out who my true self really was. Whether people love me or hate me, deep down I know that God created me this way for a reason. As long as we are being true to what we feel God wants us to do, it doesn't matter what other people think.

I believe that as long as I am loving God, and giving that love to others, I'm on the right path. And as far as my value as a human being, my popularity doesn't matter, the material possessions I own don't matter, my achievements don't matter, the "likes" I get on my posts don't matter, etc. When this life is over, I can't take any of it with me, so why should I give it so much importance? I shouldn't. And neither should you!

So let me ask you, are you living free of others' opinions of you? You *can*, and you *should*. You deserve to live this way! It doesn't matter what others say or do; nothing can change the truth about how special you are. There are plenty of people on the planet that will appreciate you and like you for you.

The truth is, your self-perception should never be tied up in what your haters say you are, or even what your biggest fans say you are. When you are being true to who you are deep down, some people will love you for it, and others might not. But that's okay! You were created this way for a good reason. You can be free of living for the opinions of others, and enjoy who you were created to be.

DAILY CHALLENGE:

Today, take a pass on tracking your likes and follows on your accounts and your concern about what people think of you. Instead, enjoy sharing time with the people you actually like being with, offline or online. Think of the ways God has specifically wired you, and be grateful for your uniqueness. Begin to think of how you can bless people in your path in ways only you can. Are there things you are doing only to impress other people? Do you actually enjoy doing those things? If anything comes to mind, write it down. If the only motive is to get validation from others, and you don't actually enjoy what you're doing, stop doing those things, and replace them with something that is true to who you really are!

DAILY INSPIRATION:

I'm not trying to win the approval of people, but of God. (Galatians 1:10 NLT)

CHAPTER 22

Life is a Gift, Enjoy It.

Stress and worry do nothing but drain you of the energy God gives you to have an incredible day.

Life is such a gift! Even though we all have our share of hardships (some more than others), and life often seems unfair, it is still a blessing, and we only get one! Have you ever really stopped to think about how short life really is? It's all going to fly by before we know it. When I was sixteen, I thought I would have everything together and all my goals accomplished by the time I turned twenty-one… and then I turned twenty-one… Whoa, was I wrong. The time went by so fast!

I think there are two different options we have when we internalize the fact that we are only here on this earth for a short period of time. We can allow it to depress us, or we can choose to let it inspire us and motivate us to make life count. I choose the second option, and I want to encourage you to do the same.

Share your heart with the world. Let love guide you.

Change lives for the better. Have fun with the life you have been given. If you aren't enjoying your time each day, then you need to reset your perspective and look for ways to bring joy to your life.

I have no idea what tomorrow will bring. Do you? Sometimes I think I do, but I really don't. What's the point in worrying about things you have absolutely no control over? Think about it: you don't need to worry about something you can control, because you can do something about it. And you don't need to worry about what you cannot control either, because there is nothing you can do!

Sometimes, I actually think we take little things too seriously, but big things not seriously enough. *Many people major in minor things.* For instance, taking seriously our likes or some comment on social media, but not seriously thinking about what matters most in life.

I have to tell you, I've learned to just laugh at myself when I mess up! I used to get so down on myself when I didn't live up to my standard, or when I would do embarrassing things. Problem was, I was fighting a bad mood more often than I wished, because things rarely always went the way I wanted them to. And the fact of the matter is, I can always find problems if I'm looking for them. Now, I've learned to just laugh when things don't go my way. I have faith in the bigger picture that I might not be able to understand or see in the present moment.

I remember times I would contemplate potential upcoming stressful situations, playing them over in my head, spending hours and hours just thinking about every possible outcome. But guess what? Those bad scenarios I played out in my head hardly ever happened!

I have to tell you a funny story (actually not so funny at

the time!). In the recent past, I was flown out by a major television network to try out for a new TV show. I was honored they wanted me in it, but I had decided I did not think it fit into my goals at that time, and was honest with them about it. Even so, they still wanted to fly me out anyway to "audition" in order to just meet the producers.

So, I agreed, with the sole purpose of meeting the producers and judges, understanding that I would not be filmed for TV since I'd already declined doing the show. So I'm out in Hollywood, having a fun time meeting all the contestants and network staff. I go up to my hotel room to get some rest before meeting the producers that night.

I kid you not, as I got in bed to lay down, my phone rang. Last minute, they said they wanted me down immediately to audition, and that I would be filmed. That's show biz for you! Immediately, I was overcome by nerves. I quickly threw on clothes and ran down to the audition room. Every possible negative scenario and outcome of doing this audition and being shown on TV started racing through my head. Let me tell you, what started out super fun turned outrageously unfun in a matter of minutes!

I was about to dip out, but I finally told myself that at the very worst case, this would be a really funny story to tell. "Don't take this too seriously," I told myself. And I have to tell you, I actually got through the audition pretty well, connected with some incredible people, and they honored my request to not appear on the show. It all worked out! I have to say looking back, I'm glad I did it, and I'm happy I chose to not overthink it and give in to fear, but decided to just lighten up and have fun!

There's an interesting acronym to remember about fear: FEAR is just False Expectations Appearing Real. There is definitely some truth to that! Instead of spending time worrying about potential negative outcomes, we should be using that energy to plan for whatever situation we are worrying about in the first place. Instead of giving into fear, use that energy to enjoy your life, and stay present to fix the problems as they come. It sounds like a simple fix, and it is simple. However, it's a choice we still have to make if we will do it or not.

I encourage you to live life with the mindset that God is working through you in ways that you might not be able to realize now, but every step you take is a step forward. As long as you give your best each day, and seek God in all you do, then you can feel good about that. It will free you to lighten up, not take the daily stuff so seriously, and enjoy your life!

Your happiness is in direct relation to your gratefulness. Gratefulness is a choice; a decision that comes from within. We can choose to be thankful, learn from, and find the best out of each moment, keeping our attention on the present. We can decide to have faith, and choose not to worry about the future.

Be free from worry today! Have faith that God is moving in and through you to fit into a bigger plan you might not be able to see right now, and then live like it! You can live your life knowing that if you are giving your best, your actions are making a positive impact, whether you see the impact immediately or not.

Life is short; it will pass you by before you know it. Stress and worry do nothing but drain you of the energy God gives you to have an incredible day. Let's remember that happiness is a choice. Let's choose to enjoy life! :)

DAILY CHALLENGE:

Grab a journal or spiral and write down the things you feel are weighing you down or robbing you of your joy. Take your worries and turn them into prayers; release them all to God, and have faith that He will work everything for good in the bigger picture of your life. Then, let them go! Set your mind on choosing happiness, with positive expectation for the blessings to come. Now, write down three things that bring you joy in the day. They can be as simple as taking the dog for a walk, or listening to your favorite song...just write down whatever comes to your mind. Do those things today. Life is too short to not take time for things you enjoy!

DAILY INSPIRATION:

Don't fret or worry. Instead of worrying, pray. Let petitions and praises shape your worries into prayers, letting God know your concerns. Before you know it, a sense of God's wholeness, everything coming together for good, will come and settle you down. It's wonderful what happens when Christ displaces worry at the center of your life. (Philippians 4:6-7 MSG)

CHAPTER 23

First Impressions Matter

The first impression you make on social media should open more doors that lead you to your ideal future, never close doors.

What's the first thing you do after you meet someone whom you find super interesting and would like to see again? You get their full name, and you try to find out more about them, right? My bet would be you would check them out on social media. No doubt, I would do that too. You get to know a lot about a person from how they represent themselves on social media.

Whether we like it or not, the way we come across on social media matters not only for our personal lives, but our professional lives also. Through our presence on social media, life-changing opportunities can be opened up for us that could be hard to make happen otherwise. Likewise, incredible opportunities can also be closed to us forever if we aren't careful. First impressions are so important. *So very important.* Even with relationships, for better or worse, we decide a lot about our feelings for a person from the first impressions they give us.

During my research about this, I found that it only takes seven seconds for a person to get a first impression about someone. We make a lot of judgements about another person consciously and subconsciously within the first seven seconds of meeting. *Do you realize how important those seven seconds are?*

Today, I believe your first impression on social media is just as important as how you come across in person. That might sound extreme, but I truly believe it, because I've seen evidence of it. I've seen friends who are now living their dream because of opportunities they received through the positive impression they gave others on social media. I also know people who had companies turn them down due to their careless social media posts, even posts made in the past.

I'll give a personal example here that relates to social media. When I first began to seriously go after my music career at age 17, I revamped my social media channels, and really gave them a professional look. I created content around my main passion at the time, which was singing. I didn't have a huge audience listening to my songs, but because I created high quality and professional content that was authentic to what I liked, a few acclaimed producers (worked with top 40 artists) took note.

But actually, what made them contact me was when they watched one of my livestreams and liked what they felt from it. They told me that they could tell I genuinely cared for those who were listening to my music and watching my broadcasts. They also could tell I was an honest guy who represented myself well through being authentic—that is why they reached out. That led me to working with an acclaimed producer from a well-known company that worked with many top artists you would recognize. Even though I didn't sign with them, that opportunity was really what started my music journey, and it all came from how I represented myself on social media.

An important question you should ask yourself frequently is, "Do my social media accounts reflect what I want to share with the world?" "Am I being authentic, while also reflecting my best self?" I ask myself these questions and similar ones all the time.

I want social media to do nothing but benefit my current relationships, and I never want my social media accounts to hinder potential positive relationships in the future. Of course, I want the same for you. Life is too short to not give ourselves the very best opportunities we can. Just don't be careless and post stuff that will not represent the best of who you are.

In fact, delete content that you feel is not reflecting your best self. I've actually removed posts I didn't feel represented my best, authentic self. Certain content I created years ago just didn't reflect me anymore. I am not saying it was terrible by any means, I just didn't think it fit who I am now and represented me well.

There is absolutely no shame in removing content that doesn't reflect the true you anymore! Don't stress at all if you need to do that. Whether you posted it three years ago, or three minutes ago, if you don't feel it represents who you authentically are or want to be, there is absolutely no reason not to remove it from your feed! In fact, I encourage you to do that.

Just want to make it clear though, in no way am I encouraging you to be over-perfectionistic about everything you post! My intention is just to get you thinking about how you can represent your very best self on social media. So when your future boyfriend, girlfriend, best friend, employer, businesses partner, manager, agent, etc., stumbles onto your social media channel, it shows them who you authentically are.

You don't want past posts to create misunderstandings about you that you will have to waste time clearing up if you don't have to. This goes for pictures people tag you in too, so definitely give this some thought. The first impression you make on social media should open *more* doors that lead you to your ideal future, never close doors.

DAILY CHALLENGE:

Today, do a quick audit of your pics and other content to make sure your feed represents the best you and the person you want to be. Feel fine deleting ones you don't like on your feed, no matter how old or new they are. You aren't obligated to keep them posted for anyone but yourself and your future opportunities. Never feel like you owe the public or anyone else any posts you feel awkward about and wish to take down.

DAILY INSPIRATION:

Whatever you do, work at it with all your heart, as working for the Lord…. (Colossians 3:23 NIV)

CHAPTER 24

Connecting With Others

For the first time in history, we are all connected at the touch of a button.

Social media has made the world such a small place. It literally blows my mind sometimes. We can communicate instantaneously with thousands of people on the other side of the world. That was unheard of even just fifteen years ago. Who knows what it will be like in the next fifteen years!

The Internet has enabled our generation to live in one big global neighborhood together. We can form friendships with others no matter where we live, and we no longer have to spend enormous amounts of money to fly to a different continent to meet people of different cultures. Our lives have the potential to be so much more enriched through relationships with others different than ourselves.

This is by far one of the most awesome things about all the progress in technology and social media: the ease of forming community with people all over the world, allowing opportunities to learn and grow. It is unreal how technology has brought us all together. For the first time in history, we are all connected at the touch of a button.

I've met so many great friends through social media connections. Some friends are in different states I have never visited, or even on the opposite side of the world, living in a completely different culture than my own.

Here is a really cool example of how you can connect all over the globe in one big community online. Awhile back on an online livestream broadcast, I asked where everyone was from. I wrote down all the states and countries represented that I saw come in on the comments, and there were over 25 U.S. states and 28 different countries! Some of these countries were in political conflict at the time, yet the individuals themselves were connecting personally as friends. How awesome is *that*? We had 28 different nations of people represented online at the same time, writing a song with me, sharing ideas, and having fun with each other. Amazing!

Now, I wouldn't be doing you right unless I talk about safety in this chapter as well. Given all the awesome connections we can make on the Internet, it can be dangerous if we aren't careful with our connections. Unfortunately, we live in a world that has proven itself to be untrustworthy regarding people we don't know.

The term "stranger danger" definitely applies on social media too, as there are twisted people out there. And trust me, some of these people are really intelligent when it comes to convincing you they are authentic. The problem is, some are dangerous and are professionals at luring innocent people to meet up, promising you things only to hurt you in the end. I really don't want this to ever be something you encounter, that is why I'm bringing this up.

Here is the bottom line: *Never, ever, ever share personal information on social media with anyone whom you have not met or confirmed to be who they say they are.* By personal information I mean where you live, your address, phone number, personal details of your life, and so forth. If you're like me, you're wired to expect people to be basically nice and honest, so your tendency might be to trust people too soon online before confirming who they are.

Just to be clear, I'm not talking about holding back kindness from people, or not allowing yourself to enjoy new friends you make on social media. I'm talking about boundaries with personal information that would be risky for you if the person turned out to be different than who they represented themselves to be. Again, make a firm rule for yourself to never be lured in any way to share personal information with anyone at any time without knowing them or verifying their identity. It's not worth the risk!

Actually, when you think about it, sharing personal stuff isn't necessary to maintain these global connections at a level you would enjoy. I have made tons of new friends online this way! And I don't expect them to share personal information with me either. It's all good!

On another note, as we focus on connecting with others and forming community, always remember the friends that are right in front of you. I know for me, if I don't have people in my life I can eat a meal with, laugh with, high-five and hug, I'd go crazy. I'm sure you can relate! All this to say, even though social media offers amazing relationships you couldn't otherwise have, make sure to take time to get to know others that live right around you!

Life is just way more fun when you live and work alongside others! Offline and online, I have realized the importance of having community the older I get. An example of this right now is the community I have with my three awesome roommates. One of them I have known since early high school, and he is like a brother to me. The other two are twin brothers I actually just met last year in a TV show audition. Because I reached back out to the twins to check in after that audition I told you about was over and everyone had gone back to their home states, we formed a friendship which led to being roommates, and that led to us collaborating with songwriting and recording. Had I never reached out to them, I would have missed out on the fun of writing and recording together, which has been an absolute blast!

In our generation, there has never been a better time in history to connect with others, and there are billions of people to choose from now! Enjoy learning from others who are from different cultures and backgrounds, and with caution, take opportunities through your social media connections to grow and develop lasting relationships.

DAILY CHALLENGE:

Today, think through the people you follow on your social media platforms, including those that live in far away places with cultures different from yours. If it sounds fun to reach out and form a friendship, send them a message today! In the same way, think of those people right around you that would be fun to hang with. Reach out to them too. This could be the start of some very special friendships that could last a lifetime, adding value to all of your lives! And of course, always set firm boundaries with the amount of personal information you share on social media. Safety should always be a priority.

DAILY INSPIRATION:

Become wise by walking with the wise. (Proverbs 13:20a MSG)

CHAPTER 25

Finding Happiness

Happiness grows inside you when you seek to give it to others.

What's the secret to happiness? That's the million-dollar question right there. I don't know if there is one "secret" to being happy all the time, but I do know something you can do right now that will make you feel ten times more content and fulfilled throughout the day. And in my experience, when you feel content, happiness will be a byproduct.

Even though I have been blessed with some great moments in my life, there have been periods of time that have brought some challenges in this area for sure, when discontentment and unhappiness would threaten my inner joy. Late in high school and my first year of college, I never realized just how much of the unhappiness I struggled with was rooted in focusing too much on myself.

I was set on everything going my way—my relationships, academics, music, fitness, career, etc. This mindset (as you can guess) led me to tons of frustration. Because I'll be real, things almost never turned out exactly the way I wanted. This left me living having to manage constantly being disappointed. Things just don't ever seem to go perfectly. You know what I mean?

It's easy to remember when it all changed for me during my freshman year at the university. There was a month where I felt like I was just losing in all areas of life. I was not performing up to par in my classes, I had to close down a new business venture, my relationships were falling apart (I wasn't being a good friend), I injured my shoulder which kept me from being able to exercise, I couldn't sleep well at night, and on and on. Just a horrible month.

Was it really though? I mean, come on, so many other people have hardships a thousand times worse. In truth, I had so much to be grateful for: my health, family, great roommates, ability to get a college degree, musical skills, etc. If you think you have it bad, I promise there is always someone who has it worse. Why couldn't I see that? I was only focused on myself. I couldn't see a bigger picture.

When I finally came to that realization, I knew I needed to change my mental perspective. I started focusing on how I could care more for others and make life better *for them*. I adopted a higher purpose than just what I wanted to happen for myself. I chose to look at my circumstances with faith that everything was happening for a reason, that there is a bigger picture that I might not be able to see right now, but it's all a part of God's plan. And when I give control back to God, focusing on what is most important, things will work out in the right time, and God will still get me where I need to be. And with this new perspective, I was able to turn everything around!

Happiness and contentment is best found outside yourself. It grows inside you when you seek to give it others. When you take your focus off yourself, you will find your joy grows inside. Think about it. So much of our dissatisfaction and disappointment with life comes from how we interpret what is happening to us, especially when things don't go the way we want them to. In reality, many times we're only focusing on ourselves, and not looking at the bigger picture.

And I totally get it—higher purpose, helping people, that sounds like the cliché answer. But I promise you, you will be so much more fulfilled and happy throughout the day when you have a higher purpose in what you do. The world does not revolve around a single person—me *or* you. That's why thinking that way does not ever ultimately fulfill, and it won't work either! Adopting a purpose greater than just living for yourself is crucial to long term happiness. You will see, as you look for ways to love and serve those around you, your happiness truly will grow.

I believe the true meaning of life is to love God and love others. However, with the craziness life brings, sometimes it's just easy to forget. Loving God and loving others seems so simple, but this is not always easy to keep in mind. Yet, when we do this, it blesses others and makes all the difference for our own happiness.

DAILY CHALLENGE:

Today, take the focus off your own problems, and write down some names of people going through a tough time that you could specifically encourage. Jot down ideas of things you could do for them—a simple text or comment, an offer to assist them in some way, or perhaps a phone call to meet and do something together. *You'll find more joy and happiness growing inside you when you are a blessing to others.*

DAILY INSPIRATION:

Be humble, thinking of others as better than yourselves. Don't look out only for your own interests, but take an interest in others, too...have the same attitude that Christ Jesus had. (Philippians 2:3-5 NLT)

CHAPTER 26

Developing an Attitude of Gratitude

Gratitude is the soil in which fulfillment and success grow strongest.

How do you define success? Having tons of money? Popularity? This is one of the most important questions to ask yourself. I see so many people in our generation who define success in one of these ways (or they have no idea how they would define it, yet they are stressing to achieve "it"). I especially see this time and time again on social media. Sure, having money and being able to provide are important, and we should all value that, don't get me wrong. And being well-liked and respected is a notable achievement. But, don't kid yourself into thinking a certain amount of money or fame will make you truly fulfilled.

I know many wealthy and financially successful individuals who don't enjoy their lives, and I'm sure you probably know some too. They may show their lives a certain way on social media, but in person, they are totally different and don't seem genuinely happy at all. In fact, sometimes it seems like the more success or fame someone gets by the world's standards, the greater their chance of depression, substance abuse, failed relationships, and more.

I've definitely felt this irony in my own life before. As weird as it sounds, I remember at one point feeling like the more I achieved, the emptier I felt. Why? The reason was because I was working out of desperation. I was trying to achieve things to fill a void inside. I was so confused why I wasn't happy after achieving what I thought would satisfy me. At one point, I stressed so much over achievement that I burned my esophagus (too many all-nighters working and lots of coffee are a bad combination). I'm glad I finally learned this lesson, even though I had to learn it the hard way. Setting goals and achieving things are noble pursuits, but they definitely will not lead to true and lasting fulfillment as an end by themselves.

In my own life, *gratitude* has been the biggest factor in feeling successful and fulfilled, not money or achievements, which is how success is popularly portrayed. Without gratitude, our human nature is to never feel satisfied—we are always wanting more.

You have a decision to make each day: A decision to choose to be grateful, or to sulk in your problems. I'll be real, no matter what you achieve, you can always find problems. As I mentioned before, I always used to think as soon as I reached this goal or that goal, I'd be satisfied. I would be my ultimate happiest. Then I achieved what I thought I wanted, and guess what? Even though it felt awesome to reach my goal, I found that after a time, I still wasn't completely satisfied.

At each milestone I reached, more problems to solve came with it, affecting my perspective about what I had just achieved. However, when I adopted an attitude of gratitude as I worked toward my goals, it revolutionized my take on success and fulfillment! Let me tell you, gratitude is the best kept secret, but it needs to be shouted from the rooftops! Being grateful is crucial to living with joy, contentment and peace that all people crave. *Gratitude is the soil in which fulfillment and success grow strongest.*

As I have researched and read about the power of gratitude, I have been amazed at all I have found. Did you know that being grateful can actually increase your grade point average? Help you sleep better? Improve your physical health as well as your mental health? Strengthen your friendships and relationships, and your overall well-being? Even writing a simple thank you note can pull you out of the blues!

The amount of gratitude you have throughout the day is directly related to how happy you'll be as a person! It's all about being thankful for even the smallest of things. Life itself is a gift. And every day, you can find little gifts to be grateful for, and that changes everything.

Okay...so how do you increase in gratitude?

I'll share with you what I do. Tell yourself ten things you are thankful for right now, and write them down if you can. It can instantly lift your mood. Having difficulty finding things to be thankful for? Thinking about how your life would be *without* something you have can help you realize how grateful you are to *have* it.

This really opens up a lot of things—loved ones, animals, your cell phone, a bed to sleep in, clothes to wear, shoes, soap and water, the list goes on. Do you realize that there are many children and adults in this world who do not have clean water to drink? I have traveled to areas of the world to serve those in extreme poverty and have experienced this first-hand. If you have easy access to drinking water, you are blessed. And here is another easy one—you are breathing! You're alive! Be joyful that you're able to live another day! We are incredibly blessed to be living in this beautiful world, and being grateful for everything we have will make all the difference.

Keep in mind that you can always find something to be thankful for. You can be thankful for so much today. Once you realize that every second you are still alive is a gift, those massive problems like how your friends, classmates or co-workers were gossiping behind your back don't seem so relevant anymore, do they? You're still living, you still have endless opportunities, so who cares about senseless gossip?

Taking it back to my first question about the definition of success, I hope I have convinced you that money or fame alone won't ultimately bring you fulfillment, but gratitude will always be a part. For myself, I'll use money and notoriety to love God and love people, but I won't dedicate my life to it.

As I am grateful for the blessings in my life, my understanding of what success is and is not really solidifies. I encourage you to adopt an attitude of gratitude, and feel how much more fulfilled you become. As you fill your heart with thankfulness, your joy and contentment in life will grow. This is true success!

DAILY CHALLENGE:

Today, do the sticky note gratitude challenge! Take a pad of sticky notes, or cut up some paper to make your own, and get a pen. Now start writing anything and everything that comes to mind that you have been blessed with and are grateful to have (including material and non-material things), using one sticky note for each thing. List everything from fun experiences to the people you love...your cell phone to your toothbrush...from the food you eat to being able to read.... you get the idea. Stick or spread out the notes on a big table or on the floor. You will be amazed at how much you have to be thankful for!

DAILY INSPIRATION:

Be thankful in all circumstances, for this is God's will for you... (Thessalonians 5:18 NLT)

CHAPTER 27

You Are What You Watch

If the content doesn't move you forward in the direction you want to go, don't watch it. If you don't agree with the creator's values, don't follow.

Looking back at history, I have never understood how massive groups of people could be so blind to the cruelties of their actions. How entire countries could do such terrible things to other nations, or even within their own country's borders...to other races...to other genders...to other humans. I've never understood it. How could so many people, who were probably once cute little kids with a lot of promise, become so lost as to do such horrible acts? It all goes back to the influences they had during their formative years and beyond.

Here's the thing. We are all highly influenced by our environment, even more than we dare to think, and definitely more than we would like to admit to other people, or even to ourselves. Whether we admit it or not, we reflect the people and environments we spend the most time with.

You may have heard it said that you are the average of the five people you hang out with the most. I want to add a new perspective to this idea. More than likely, you're not going to hang around people who are extremely negative, dramatic, or who will do anything no matter what to get more and more attention. I'm going to assume that you would stop hanging out with those people. But wait a second—what about the content creators you watch online?

Obviously, the people we physically spend time with in our personal lives have a massive impact on how we live. That advice is out everywhere. But, what about the people we spend time with digitally? I strongly believe that the people you consistently watch on YouTube or other platforms have the same effect on you as those you physically surround yourself with in real life.

Never underestimate the influence that the people you follow online have on you. It is different than it used to be. When I was growing up, I'd watch certain shows on TV for entertainment (which were obviously scripted and rated), and vlogging hadn't hit the scene on YouTube. I wasn't watching the crazy parts of someone's life every day for twenty minutes. The entertainment I watched didn't have that personal connection it does now.

Entertainment isn't just entertainment anymore. This is really important to understand. Content creators you watch on social media are literally like your friends now. We get access into their lives (or the life they choose to show). I bet many of you spend even more time with them than you do with your friends in person sometimes. They have the power to influence us just as much, if not more, than our school, team, colleagues or other friends do.

Here's the kicker: The intentions of a lot of popular creators is not to improve your life, it's to do whatever it takes to get you to watch their lives. Not everyone, but sadly more than you would think, do this: More eyeballs equals more money and fame. I feel our generation doesn't realize the influence the creators they watch have on them. Most just think it's "entertainment." Don't fool yourself, you are becoming more and more like the "entertainment" you watch every day.

Let me warn you, you never realize how you've been negatively influenced until it happens. It is always in retrospect. Around my junior year of high school, there was a time period where I began to act like a different person, a person my true self wouldn't like so much. You know how it happened? I got caught up in watching entertainment that promoted materialism, using others, doing anything for attention, etc.

It all stemmed from the shows I was watching on the YouTube channels I was subscribed to. I didn't intend for that content to affect me, I just found it interesting and was lured in by the charisma of the creators. But it couldn't help having an effect on me. Of course it would, if I was giving them so much of my undivided attention and interest! I think at some point I must have started to adopt the same thought patterns as they portrayed, which affected my personality. I never consciously decided to, it just happened.

After figuring out that my good friends didn't want to be around me as much anymore (I certainly wasn't as much fun to be around for sure!), I finally realized how I had changed. I missed the old me too! I snapped out of it, stopped giving that content my time, and came back to center, to who I really was.

The crazy thing is, "shock jock" and drama-filled content can be very addictive. And because it "gets the views," popular creators keep making it. It's almost like a game of who can be the most wild, or who can be the most shocking. Don't give it your attention and time— protect your heart and mind from wasting your time on watching stuff that can drag you down or take you off course. This goes for offline too, with the friends you choose to hang out with or have over. Choose wisely!

Be careful with what your eyes consume. I audit and carefully take inventory of all the entertainment I watch. Basically, if what I'm watching is not in line with my values, I turn it off. If the content doesn't move me forward in the direction I want to go, I don't watch it. If I don't agree with the creator's values, I don't follow.

All in all, just understand that whether you realize it now or not, you are becoming more and more like the attitudes and actions of the creators you watch every day. Choose the ones you will view wisely. There are many quality creators out there worth watching and being inspired by, you just have to look for them. But skip over the others who don't affirm your goals and stay true to the best version of you.

DAILY CHALLENGE:

This week, take a serious audit of the content you watch regularly, and the creators you are giving most of your time and attention to. Ask yourself if their values agree with yours, and if their content and words encourage you to be the best version of yourself. If the answer is no, then stop giving them your precious time to influence you. Instead, if you are going to spend time watching content online, watch the creators that will inspire and motivate you to be the person you want to be.

DAILY INSPIRATION:

Bad company corrupts good character. (1 Corinthians 15:33 NLT)

CHAPTER 28

Don't Be Afraid to Fail

There is no such thing as failure if you view it as an opportunity for growth.

I s there really such a thing as failure the way we often think of it? What does the word "failure" actually mean anyway? The official definition of failure is "lack of success," or "the omission of expected or required action." Basically, it means not achieving some form of success or not achieving the expected or desired outcome. If that's the case, then let me tell you—I've failed at so many things in my life. I have definitely worked hard for things, hoping for a certain outcome, and got a different one. But does this mean I am a failure?

I played for a state championship soccer team in high school. On my previous team, I was the best player, but once I moved up to the most competitive league in the highest division my junior year, I got a new status pretty fast—benched. With these incredible players, most of them seniors, I was no longer the best one, but one of the least skilled comparatively. I felt like my team and coach looked down on me. I remember losing the ball in early practices or games, and the coach would just scream and scream. At the time, I felt like a failure. It was especially hard since it was my skill and expertise that got me on this top team, but compared to the others, my performance seemed below par. I wanted to quit.

But fortunately, I decided to change my perspective. Instead of letting my mistakes lead me to quitting, I decided I was going to learn as much as I could from the other teammates and allow them to better myself on and off the field. I increased my skills, but honestly one of the best lessons I took from that season was learning how to deal with criticism. I learned many important lessons I would never have learned if I had quit.

Success or failure is all in how we perceive the outcomes we experience. It's all determined by our attitude about them. What if we replaced the word "fail" with the word "learn?" If you're learning you're improving. You're moving forward. That sounds like a success to me. Have you learned from your past mistakes? If so, they have contributed to the person you are today.

There is no such thing as failure if you view it as an opportunity for growth. Either we succeed at our original endeavor, or we learn to better ourselves for next time. Learning what not to do is also success. When you step out of your comfort zone, whether you get the outcome you wanted or not, you win regardless. You learn regardless. You succeed regardless.

I constantly have to remind myself to not let fear of failing hold me back from trying new, exciting things. I've had many messages from people asking me how they can get over their fears of sharing their passions on social media. Many artists, singers, dancers, speakers, musicians, athletes, writers and other creatives have this incredible talent they want to share with the world, but they are afraid of the rejection that might come with it. They are afraid of failing.

I know exactly how that feels, and I wouldn't be real with you if I said I don't still get nervous when I post up a new song I have recorded, or a music video I have produced. Even when I first released that I was writing this book, deep down I had a fear of people doubting me. People know me as a singer and musician, but they may wonder, who is this author? At first, I was super nervous about how people would react.

But I did it anyway. The fear was present, but I did not give into it. Instead, I re-interpreted it as an opportunity to work hard toward a new goal that I knew God put on my heart, and that I would always be nudged to do in the back of my mind until I did it. Plus, the response I've received has been incredible! What I had feared didn't even happen.

Here's the thing, you're never going to get rid of fear trying to distract you. And risking rejection never sounds good either. But don't let those feelings stop you from sharing your heart, trying new things, showcasing your talent, pursuing your goals or your ideal career, and learning along the way. If you just push through the fear, God will use it in your life to grow you, and you will make it to the other side feeling more alive and empowered to succeed than ever before.

I would like to encourage you to replace the word "failing" with words like "learning" or "experimenting." So much of your life is based on your perception of the world, and too many times, the voice of fear in your head puts unnecessary limits on your potential. You were created by God to do extraordinary things! You are a light to this world. *You cannot let fear darken that light.* Push past the initial feeling of fear, because the other side is full of growth and learning that will be another step toward your dreams.

DAILY CHALLENGE:

Is there something you have been wanting to do, but fear of failure or rejection has been holding you back? Take a chance today and try something new! Even something small. Just do something today that gets you out of your comfort zone. Push through the fear, and then tell yourself no matter what the outcome, you'll learn from it no matter what, and be better for having tried. Now that is definitely a success!

DAILY INSPIRATION:

Don't be afraid, for I am with you. Don't be discouraged, for I am your God. I will strengthen you and help you. I will hold you up with my victorious right hand. (Isaiah 41:10 NLT)

CHAPTER 29

Do Looks Matter?

God created you unique — you are beautifully made.

D o looks matter? Before I jump into this one... let me be honest with you... When I look in the mirror, I see so many things I wish I could change. Even though I've learned to embrace all the imperfections now, when I was younger my appearance was one of my biggest insecurities. In this chapter, I'm going to tell you my view on appearance and what I believe is true about it.

I can be around a girl who has "magazine perfect" looks, but if she is rude or arrogant, it's amazing how fast she turns not-so-pretty. Or you might find a guy super attractive, but when he is disrespectful and condescending, I'm sure he would become unattractive pretty quickly.

On the flip side, someone who may not have the physical attributes that our society (or rather, Hollywood) would consider pretty (which are ridiculous and unattainable standards), can turn into an absolute beauty when her heart of gold shines through in her words and actions, or when her spirit radiates pure beauty from within.

True beauty doesn't start on the surface and work inward, instead, true beauty originates from within and shines out of a person. Our current culture may tell you otherwise, but I disagree.

I try to never think too hard about what I look like when I meet people and engage with them, instead I try to focus on my heart and making sure I value them, seeking ways to build them up. I want people to feel happier and more encouraged after being with me than they were before they were with me. I know that is what is most attractive anyway, and most valued by others. Remember this: *people will forget what you looked like, but they won't forget how you made them feel.*

Now I'm not saying this perspective is easy to come by at all—it's tough! All of us have insecurities about how we look. Contrary to popular belief, the more attention you get on social media, the more magnified these insecurities often become. They don't magically go away.

If you are focused on your looks when you are with others, that will come across to them. They can feel it in the energy, or "vibe", you give off. Most people couldn't care less about your looks, but they do care about your character and how they feel when they are around you. Come to think of it, people don't usually put a priority on someone else's appearance, but they will care if that person cares!

Let's be real, social media makes it even harder to deal with common insecurities, since everything is so magnified. All it takes is one glance at the Explore page, and I'm sure you'll know what I mean. One glance, and I see people I wish I looked like, I wish I was friends with, I wish I had a feature they possess, or I wish I had something they had. I've

talked about comparison a lot in this book, but it's worth repeating, because it is such a big pain point in our culture. Social media can be a confidence killer—especially when it
comes to appearance.

So, does appearance matter? It only matters if you think it
does. Let me explain. If I go into interactions with others
thinking to myself that I don't look good, or that people will
not think I'm attractive for whatever reason, the problem
actually is not my appearance...The problem is that I'm thinking about myself instead of enjoying the people around me!
If I am preoccupied with myself, I am not present with the
other people, and that will be what is a turnoff to them, not
that my hair was messy. You get what I'm saying?

What really matters to most people is what is on the inside of a person. Maybe a few people care only about "magazine perfect" appearance, but in that case, I would encourage
you to find friends who look deeper. Your positivity, your loving heart, your confidence in yourself and other people, *that
is what is most attractive.* Your warmth and relatability, and
the connection you create with others when you are genuinely interested in them and authentically being you, this is
what truly draws people. Inner beauty is what it's all about!

DAILY CHALLENGE:

Make a list today of all the qualities you have that make you
unique. Let this bring you confidence to replace any insecurities you might have regarding your appearance or comparing
yourself to others. List some ways you can radiate your
unique inner beauty outward to bless others! Write in another section the character qualities you see in others that you

want to be true for you, and commit to start working toward developing those traits. True beauty shines first from the inside!

DAILY INSPIRATION:

The Lord does not look at the things people look at. People look at the outward appearance, but the Lord looks at the heart. (1 Samuel 16:7b NIV)

CHAPTER 30

Take a Stand

If you stand for nothing, you'll fall for anything.

If you stand for nothing, you'll fall for anything...this is profound when you really think about it! There are so many opinions out there. So many people posting, trying to sell their humor, their ideas, their values, their products, their fitness, and so on. So many marketers trying to manipulate our decisions. So much information available, and no filter to know whether it is reliable.

Social media platforms have opened the floodgates for all this, saturating our generation 24/7 with temptations and lures to adapt to whatever others say and do. And now it is to the point where we don't even have time to find our own voice in all the noise.

Today, it is easier than ever to slip up. It is easier than ever to be passively persuaded for the worse. I'm only saying this because I too have felt the persuasive power of society trying to lead me to places I never would intentionally go. Can you relate? I am so grateful I have been able to catch myself before these things could have messed up my life, and I want you to be able to as well.

I want to share with you something I do that is a big reason I have stayed on my path over the years: I take a stand for what is important to me. I think through and write out my values. I get that this might sound corny, but it has saved me over the years! This is really so important in being true to your best self.

Here is what I do: I carve out a good amount of time, and get a paper and pen, and I write out the values I want to guide my life. Then, I write out a sentence or two (typically called a mission statement) that sums up the kind of person I want to be. I save the paper in a special place, and use it to guide my important decisions.

Here is an example of my mission statement. Yours will be different, but this might give you some ideas:

My Current Personal Mission Statement:

"To influence people in my generation to live life to the full, helping them know their worth to God, encouraging them to reach their full potential, and empowering them to do the same for others."

The core values I commit to living by:
LOVE
ENCOURAGEMENT
COMPASSION
GRATITUDE
KINDNESS
COURAGE
HONESTY

INTEGRITY
DISCIPLINE
SERVICE
INFLUENCE

To this day, I have a piece of paper with my mission and these values handwritten on it. I look at it from time to time, and I update it to reflect new convictions if I need to. When I am at a decision point, I will ask myself, "Is this helping me love people better? Is this in line with integrity and representing myself in an honest way? Is this encouraging and compassionate toward people? Is this aligned with helping others know their amazing worth to God?"

My values and mission have evolved over the years, and that is totally okay. You don't need to feel any pressure to pick the perfect mission statement now, because you can always change it as you grow and learn. And you can add values to your list any time. The important thing is you have something to go back to that represents your heart and the true you, since your circumstances and peer pressure can tend to lure you from your personal mission in subtle ways when you are unaware.

Let me tell you, I am so thankful that I have made an effort to figure out what my life mission is, and on what truths I want to build my life. I urge you to do the same. And it is important that they be your personal values, not a copy of someone else's. Although my parents and other mentors in my life have helped shape my values, my mission statement needs to be my own, not written by anyone else but me, so it can be a true reflection of my convictions and what is important to me. Then, I make every effort to live these values out.

If you haven't already, you are going to have tough decisions ahead of you. There will be many forks in the road, and the best path won't always be clear at first. It is good to remind yourself of what you stand for, and what is really important to you for the long haul as you face these choices. Doing this will save you from a lot of stupid decisions, trust me!

And always remember, sometimes the *best* path is not the *easiest.* Sometimes making the right decision is extremely difficult, and you may not want to do it at first, but always know that you will never regret standing up for what you know is right.

Above all, be courageous and stay on course! You *can* make a positive difference in this world. I know you have it in you, and there is nothing like the feeling of staying true to your best self with the gifts and passions God has put inside you, no matter what.

So I will leave you with this: Take time to figure out the values you want driving your life forward. Figure out the kind of person you want to be, and stand for something. It is so easy to make time for everything else but this, and this is what is most important!

DAILY CHALLENGE:

Take some time to write your personal mission statement, including the values you want driving your life. Pick some strong ones. Handwrite or print it out, and put the paper somewhere you can find when you want to review it. Commit to courageously living these out daily, and review when making difficult decisions. You will feel so good inside knowing you are a person on a mission to make a positive difference in the world!

DAILY INSPIRATION:

Be on guard. Stand firm in the faith. Be courageous. Be strong. (1 Corinthians 16:13 NLT)

Share the Blessings!

Thank you so much for supporting my book's message and mission! Hopefully you've felt lots of love and encouragement throughout each chapter, and that every reading has given you a refreshing perspective on how to stay true to the amazing person God made you to be. I also hope the book has helped to increase your joy, peace, and confidence in yourself and your relationships on and off social media.

Deep down, I truly believe that on this earth our highest calling is to love God and love others the best we can, and to share positive, beneficial information we have learned with others to make an impact on someone else's life. That is my final challenge to you!

As you learn and experience things that make your life better, make sure to pass that knowledge on to others. What you have learned in this book, make sure to share it with friends who could really use the encouragement. More than ever before, it's so important that people of our generation know that we have each other's back. We don't have to go through life alone, and we all go through the same struggles and challenges.

I believe in you! Be a difference-maker! It will happen one life at a time. It starts with you. It starts with me. Reach out to others first, be a life-giving friend. You will never fully know the incredible impact you will have on people's lives just by confidently walking in the purpose and blessing God has for your life, and staying true to the best version of you, no matter what others do or think.

And equally important, spread this blessing to others! Share the love and the message of this book with your friends, so together we can turn this social media-obsessed generation into a life-giving force in the world!

All the best,

Justin :)

P.S. Stay in touch with me!

You can search my handle, @iamjustinburke, for most everything...Instagram, Facebook public page, Twitter, Snapchat, Musical.ly and Live.ly. My YouTube is Justin Burke. I post alerts when I will be livestreaming, and I would love for you to join my community!

My website is www.JustinBurke.co, and it will have links to all platforms and events, as well as links to my music on Spotify, Apple Music, iTunes, and other music apps.

Acknowledgements

I want to thank my mom and dad, Kathy and John Burke, for their incredible love and support! I am so blessed to have such faithful and dedicated parents believing in me and cheering me on. They have not only been mentors in my life, but my best friends, and the wisdom I have gained from their influence is reflected in these pages I have written. Mom and Dad, thank you for pouring into me. Love you both!

I am also super thankful for my big sister Ashley, whose creative gifts have been such a blessing with the initial project layout for the title and book cover design. She's also been a loyal mentor and best friend to me since the day I was born, and continues to encourage me to be the best version of me I can be. Love you so much, Ash!

I am so very grateful to my awesome Aunt Kayla, who jumped on board with her incredible talent, going above and beyond to help me make the cover exactly the way I dreamed it could be. Love you lots, Kayla!

Finally, thank you to my incredible social media family. You all bless me in ways that you couldn't even imagine! From the bottom of my heart, thank you for being a part of spreading the message in this book, and being a positive light in this world. So much love for all of you!

About the Author

Justin Burke is a 21-year old charted singer-songwriter, speaker, university student and social media personality from Austin, Texas. Beginning with YouTube at age 11, Justin has grown as a creator, musician, writer and producer. Through his original music and content, Justin has grown a community of over 1.5 million followers and over 100 million views across his social media platforms. He is a host for a popular live stream TV show where he performs his original music, leads songwriting sessions, and gives advice and encouragement. Most importantly, Justin's passion is to encourage his generation to find their worth and value in who God uniquely created them to be, use their influence on social media to spread kindness and love, and courageously make a positive difference in the world.

Reach Justin Burke on social media:
Instagram: @iamJustinBurke
Musical.ly: @iamJustinBurke
Twitter: @iamJustinBurke
Snapchat: @iamJustinBurke
Facebook: @iamJustinBurke
YouTube: "Justin Burke"

For speaking and event inquiries, please contact Justin's team on the booking inquiry link at www. JustinBurke.co.

59614374R00083

Made in the USA
Columbia, SC
05 June 2019